THE
NATIONAL
PARKS
COOKBOOK

The Best Recipes from (and Inspired by)
America's National Parks

Linda Ly

**PHOTOGRAPHY BY
WILL TAYLOR**

HARVARD
COMMON
PRESS

To Gemma Lumen and Ember Luna, our favorite people in the world. You two make old adventures new (and so very fun) again.

From the Olympic Peninsula to the Colorado Plateau, watching you both dance in the RV, wave at bison and bears from the windows, build sandcastles in deep river canyons, splash in freezing alpine lakes, soak in steamy hot springs, go on your first creek walks, forage for berries and Indian paintbrushes, and make wildflower bouquets on your hikes were the highlights of our year. We're beyond blessed to be able to call that "work" and spend the summer exploring with Wanda while collecting endless inspiration for this book (and future trips).

Here's to a life led by passion, courage, curiosity, and kindness and many more stamps in your national parks passports.

Love, Mama and Ba

Quarto.com

© 2022 Quarto Publishing Group USA Inc.
Text © 2022 Linda Ly Taylor

First Published in 2022 by The Harvard Common Press, an imprint of The Quarto Group,
100 Cummings Center, Suite 265-D, Beverly, MA 01915, USA.
T (978) 282-9590 F (978) 283-2742

The Harvard Common Press titles are also available at discount for retail, wholesale, promotional, and bulk purchase. For details, contact the Special Sales Manager by email at specialsales@quarto.com or by mail at The Quarto Group, Attn: Special Sales Manager, 100 Cummings Center, Suite 265-D, Beverly, MA 01915, USA.

27 26 25 24 23   2 3 4 5

ISBN: 978-0-7603-7511-2

Digital edition published in 2022
eISBN: 978-0-7603-7512-9

Library of Congress Control Number: 2022937691

Design and Page Layout: Amy Sly
Cover Image: Will Taylor
Photography: Will Taylor

Printed in China

PREFACE

The first national park I ever visited was the Grand Canyon. I was too young to remember much from that trip—but building memories that a kid might remember isn't the real reason for taking your little ones on trips. That first visit offered something more: It planted a deep-rooted appreciation for the outdoors, for being with family, and for road trips and endless exploration throughout my adulthood.

Dozens of national parks later, those experiences have been some of the most fun (and transcendental moments) in my life. I checked off six national parks while writing *The New Camp Cookbook* with a newborn in tow, and when I took on *The National Parks Cookbook*, I saw it as another amazing opportunity to travel for work, this time with baby number two on board. My husband, the kids, and I piled into the RV and set off for an entire summer of researching and photographing as many national parks as we could, adding eleven parks and eight states to our itinerary.

But summer 2021 was a weird time for travel. Parks were requiring reservations just to enter the gates, most lodges were operating at half capacity or closed completely, and the food . . . well, let's just say limited menus and lukewarm takeout didn't exactly equal cookbook inspiration. And it's certainly a disappointment for the average family that can carve out a visit only once a year.

That, partly, is why this book exists. Sometimes, life (or crazy world circumstances) gets in the way and travel gets a lot trickier. Or, maybe it's the depth of winter and you're itching to re-create your favorite meals at home while dreaming of summer holidays. Maybe you want to keep this book on your coffee table to rediscover childhood adventures, motivate yourself to start planning that trip you've always wanted to take, or learn about parks that have previously flown under your radar.

Ultimately, I wrote this book to share the sights, smells, and flavors of the national parks with people who can't get away (or get away as often as they'd like). You'll find a sliver of history in these pages along with recipes inspired by the flora and fauna of the parks, regional specialties with interesting back stories, recipes reenvisioned from meals I've enjoyed in the lodges over the years, and dishes contributed by well-loved dining rooms and chefs. My hope is that whether or not you make it to a national park this year, you can still get your national park fix, even from hundreds or thousands of miles away.

CONTENTS

Yellowstone National Park

NATIONAL PARKS OF ALASKA

INTRODUCTION

It all started around a campfire. (Maybe.)

Everybody loves a good campfire story, and like many campfire stories fueled by one too many drinks and woven with urban legend, the story of how national parks came to be has all the elements of a great myth: intrepid explorers sitting around the glow of a campfire, discussing hopes and dreams and, ultimately, pursuing what's widely been called "America's best idea."

The story goes like this: In the late nineteenth century, the Washburn–Langford–Doane Expedition traveled south from Montana into the region we know today as Yellowstone National Park. The group included a surveyor-general, a businessman, and an attorney; they wanted to witness for themselves what earlier explorers had described as a peculiar collection of spouting water, steaming rivers, and boiling bubbling mud.

In August and September of 1870, the expedition stumbled upon all that and more, mapping and recording the Grand Canyon of the Yellowstone, Yellowstone Falls, and Old Faithful. As the men settled into camp near the confluence of the Gibbon and Firehole rivers, overwhelmed by what they'd seen, the conversation around the campfire turned to how this wondrous area might be divided among the group's profit-minded entrepreneurs.

But one member, an attorney named Cornelius Hedges, suggested a higher purpose: that there be no private ownership of the land, that its features were so exceptional they had to be preserved for all to see. It was an unusual proposal at the time, but the idea caught on and less than two years later, Yellowstone National Park was created on March 1, 1872, "for the benefit and enjoyment of the people"—an inscription that can be seen today atop the Roosevelt Arch, which spans the northern entrance to Yellowstone.

How much of this story is true has been debated by historians, but we do know one thing: Yellowstone *was* saved from private development, and it inspired a century of advocacy in protecting the nation's natural resources and landmarks. Where wilderness was once just "the place Indians were," it was now a sanctuary, an escape from urbanization, and a sacred place where Indigenous cultures were preserved and honored.

As national parks expanded from west to east, and weeks-long rail travel gave way to weekend car trips, more and more people were able to experience the majesty of the mountains that was once reserved exclusively for the upper class. Iconic lodges like Old Faithful Inn, The Ahwahnee hotel, and Glacier Park Lodge provided oases of civilization in remote and rugged areas. They became the

Yellowstone National Park

People visit the national parks to feel a kinship with nature. It's a journey that offers a feast for the senses—from the smell of wildflowers in Mt. Rainier's meadows to the sound of birds echoing off Zion Canyon.

core of the national park experience—one where people, food, and landscapes were virtually inseparable.

People visit the national parks to feel a kinship with nature. It's a journey that offers a feast for the senses—from the smell of wildflowers in Mt. Rainier's meadows to the sound of birds echoing off Zion Canyon.

But food is what provides a framework for the human experience. A traveler's fondest memories might include picking sun-ripened peaches from the orchards at Capitol Reef National Park to put in a campfire cobbler, sipping huckleberry cocktails while watching the sunset from the deck of Jackson Lake Lodge, or savoring a farm-to-fork dinner with

sweeping views of the Shenandoah Valley from the Pollock Dining Room at Skyland.

Food has long been an important part of our heritage, and in *The National Parks Cookbook*, you'll read about national park lodges and restaurants that have worked to preserve their agricultural and culinary traditions—some that go back a hundred years. You'll re-create signature dishes you remember from your visits, even some from your childhood. And you'll find that the bounty of the land lends itself to a number of recipes that help bring the flavors of the national parks into your home.

Glacier National Park

KITCHEN ESSENTIALS AND KNOW-HOW

You don't need a fancy kitchen to whip up delicious meals like a chef.

The National Parks Cookbook was created with the home cook in mind, adapting high-volume restaurant recipes to scaled-down versions suitable for a family. That means you can use the same tools and ingredients you've always used—no unusual gadgets collecting dust after one meal, or gallon-size jugs of powdered chicken base to buy and store. This chapter outlines what I use throughout the book and the brands suggested are everyday brands I like and trust (found in stores nationwide).

TOOLS

You can use ordinary kitchen equipment to turn out extraordinary food, just like you remember from your national park visits. Along with the saucepans and skillets in the following chart, a few recipes also call for a cast-iron skillet (though any heavy-bottom ovenproof skillet with tall sides will work).

STANDARD COOKING VESSEL SIZES

	Saucepan	Skillet
Small	1 to 1½ quarts (960 ml to 1.4 L)	8 inches (20 cm)
Medium	2 to 3 quarts (1.9 to 2.8 L)	10 inches (25 cm)
Large	4 quarts (3.8 L)	12 inches (30 cm)

A stockpot or "large pot" should hold 5 quarts (4.8 L) or more, and a Dutch oven is a large pot that's wider than it is deep (I recommend at least 6 quarts, or 5.8 L). For recipes that call for deep-frying, use any heavy pan (such as a sauté pan, rondeau pan, or braiser) that's at least 3 inches (7.5 cm) deep.

Food processor: A food processor makes quick work of mixing dough, shredding blocks of cheese, or breaking down a lot of food at one time. I use an 11-cup (2.6 L) Cuisinart, but if you don't have the space for a full-size food processor, I suggest a midsize 6- to 8-cup (1.4 to 1.9 L) model for more versatility.

High-powered blender: A good-quality, high-speed blender will help you achieve the smoothest results for purees and sauces.

Immersion blender: When you need to puree something (for example, soup), it's much easier to puree right in the pot than to transfer the liquid to and from a blender. A variable-speed immersion blender (also called a hand blender or stick blender) is a good investment if you make a lot of creamy soups (like Virginia Peanut Soup, page 148), sauces, dips, and dressings.

Kitchen scale: A scale is the unsung hero of a kitchen. Although you might never strictly need it, when you do use it, you inevitably become a better cook. I recommend a compact digital scale that weighs in pounds/ounces as well as kilograms/grams and has a capacity

up to 11 pounds (5 kg), which is sufficient for most cooks. The Escali brand has been a workhorse in my kitchen for years.

Loaf pan: I recommend a standard bread loaf pan (9 × 5 inches, or 23 × 13 cm) made of heavyweight aluminized steel for excellent heat conductivity and durability.

Microplane zester: For zesting citrus peels or grating garlic or ginger, I like to use my Microplane (rasp-style grater), which produces evenly sized shreds.

Pie pan: Pie pans (often called pie plates) come in a range of materials including aluminum, ceramic, and glass; any of those will work. Unless specified otherwise, the recipes in this book use a standard 9-inch (23 cm) size.

Popover pan: I prefer to use a standard 6-cup (1.4 L) popover pan for my Perfect Popovers (page 63), as the narrow cups with straight sides help the popovers really *pop* out of the pan and balloon over the edges. You can use a muffin pan in a pinch, but the size and shape of your popovers won't be the same.

Rolling pin: Rolling pins come in many shapes, sizes, and materials; use any style you're comfortable with.

Sheet pan: Sheet pans are also known as rimmed baking sheets. The best ones are made of heavy-gauge aluminum that doesn't warp under high heat. Sizes I use most often are "half sheets" (18 × 13 inches, or 20 × 33 cm) and "quarter sheets" (13 × 9 inches, or 33 × 23 cm) with 1-inch (2.5 cm)-tall sides. I recommend the Nordic Ware brand.

Springform pan: A standard 9-inch (23 cm) springform pan has a removable bottom and sides that clinch together with a clip. This type of pan is essential for the Wild Game Savory Cheesecake with Alaskan King Crab Mustard Sauce (page 171), so it removes easily after setting.

Stand mixer: Certain recipes call for a stand mixer, but if you don't have one, your next best option is a handheld mixer with interchangeable attachments for mixing and whipping. You can also mix, whip, and knead by hand, but doing so will take a bit more strength and stamina.

Tart pan: A standard 9-inch (23 cm) tart pan has fluted edges and a removable bottom for easy serving of your fruit tarts (like the Blueberry and Salmonberry Frangipane Tart, page 192).

Thermometer: A candy thermometer is essential for deep-frying, though many digital instant-read thermometers (that you typically use for meat) can also be used to determine oil temperature. Check the manual that came with your meat thermometer before using it for oil. I use and love the Thermapen from ThermoWorks.

INGREDIENTS

The recipes in this book rely on a handful of pantry staples, and I list exactly what I use to provide consistency in taste and measurement. When working with your own brands and ingredients, use your best judgment and keep in mind important things like the size of the grain, amount of salt, level of sweetness, or fat content that may alter how your dish turns out.

Broth: I almost always use broth or stock made from chicken or beef, but you can substitute vegetable broth (just keep in mind the flavor will be a bit different). Whether you make your own or use store-bought, it's assumed your broth or stock is already well-seasoned. If it isn't, you may need to add more salt than the recipe calls for.

Butter: For all of my cooking and baking, I use salted butter. I rotate among common supermarket brands, but the average stick (8 tablespoons, or 112 g) of salted butter that I buy contains about ¼ teaspoon salt. If you prefer unsalted butter, you may need to adjust the amount of salt called for in the recipe, especially if it requires ¼ cup (56 g) of butter or more. (Anything less and you likely won't taste a difference.)

Eggs: Egg size is always large. Whenever possible, I encourage you to buy pasture-raised eggs (as opposed to free-range, cage-free, or vegetarian-fed eggs). If you don't have a local source, Vital Farms (found in well-stocked supermarkets) is an ethical brand I like.

Flour: Unless specified otherwise, all recipes that call for flour use Gold Medal unbleached all-purpose flour, a middle-of-the-range flour with 10.5 percent gluten. Keep in mind that different brands of all-purpose flours have varying gluten content, especially across regions, so use your best judgment if you feel your dough needs more or less liquid to hold its shape.

Milk and other dairy: Milk is always whole and other dairy products, such as sour cream or cream cheese, are full fat. Using skim or low-fat dairy may affect the outcome of recipes that rely on the fat content for proper results.

Nonstick cooking spray: Avocado oil spray is a workhorse in my kitchen, as it's a healthier alternative to traditional cooking sprays and has a neutral flavor and high smoke point. I like the Chosen Foods brand, which is available in most grocers.

Olive oil: For day-to-day cooking, I recommend an inexpensive, light and fruity extra-virgin olive oil. For drizzling over dishes or whisking into dressings, I prefer a rich and robust extra-virgin olive oil. My favorite brands are California Olive Ranch and Kirkland Signature (Costco brand), as the oils are always fresh and flavorful. If you're feeling overwhelmed by the selection in the store, choose a cold-pressed extra-virgin olive oil sold in a dark bottle, which helps prevent oxidation.

Salt: In all recipes, I use Morton coarse kosher salt. If you don't use this same brand, think of the measurement as a reference point when seasoning with salt. For example, if you use fine-grain crystals, start by halving the amount of salt called for in the recipes and then add more to taste.

Sugar: Unless specified otherwise, all sugar is C&H pure cane sugar (white granulated sugar).

Vegetable oil: Vegetable oil is specified in recipes that require an oil with a neutral flavor or high smoke point. I like to use sunflower oil or avocado oil for deep-frying, pan-frying, and stir-frying. My go-to brands are Napa Valley Naturals, Chosen Foods, and La Tourangelle. For deep-frying, you can buy an economical gallon jug of sunflower oil from Azure Standard, an online grocery co-op.

Wine: When a recipe calls for white wine, any midrange dry white wine will do; I prefer Pinot Grigio. For a dry red wine, my go-tos are Cabernet Sauvignon, Merlot, or Malbec. Never use a bottle labeled "cooking wine," as it's bottom-of-the-barrel wine to which salt and food coloring have been added. Using a wine you like to drink will always make your recipe taste better.

STANDARDS AND TECHNIQUES

Sometimes, it's the little things that can save you time, clear up uncertainty, or otherwise make the meal easier to throw together. Here are a few key points to keep in mind as you work your way through the recipes.

Herbs and spices: A "sprig" (of any herb) is an approximate 4-inch (10 cm) piece of the herb stem. If you don't have fresh herbs available, you can generally substitute dried herbs. A good rule is 1 teaspoon of dried equals 1 tablespoon (weight varies) of fresh. Dried herbs and spices do have an optimal shelf life, so if yours have been sitting around for a while, you may need to use a little more to get good flavor.

Measuring flour: In this book, flour is measured without sifting it first. I use the "scoop and sweep" method for measuring flour: scoop a heaping mound of flour in my measuring cup, then sweep a straightedge across the cup to level it. Do not tamp down on the flour or tap the cup on a surface to settle it. If your flour has been compacted at the bottom of a bag or canister, lightly fluff it with a fork before scooping.

Peeling: Simply put, I don't do it for things like carrots and potatoes, because peeling strips away the vegetable's nutritional benefits and has little effect on texture. You can peel vegetables for aesthetic reasons, but it isn't necessary as long as your produce is washed well.

Salting: Recipes throughout this book call for specific amounts of salt during prepping or cooking to disgorge or enhance the ingredients. Because salting is subjective, feel free to add more at the end of the recipe if you feel the dish still needs it.

Toasting nuts: Because toasting times vary widely depending on the size of the nuts and the accuracy of your oven, I prefer to use the dry pan method. For toasting small quantities of nuts, it's the surest way to keep them from browning (or burning) too quickly.

Start by heating a small skillet over medium heat. (No fat is needed; you want the skillet dry.) Spread the nuts across the surface and toast, stirring occasionally, until they release a rich and nutty fragrance. You want a golden brown or slightly darker color overall but never any black spots.

Vegetables: Unless quantities are specified by weight or volume, assume all vegetables (including garlic cloves) to be medium, or average, in size. "Medium" can be an ambiguous term, but if I feel a little more or a little less won't make or break the dish, I simply call for a basic whole quantity in my recipes.

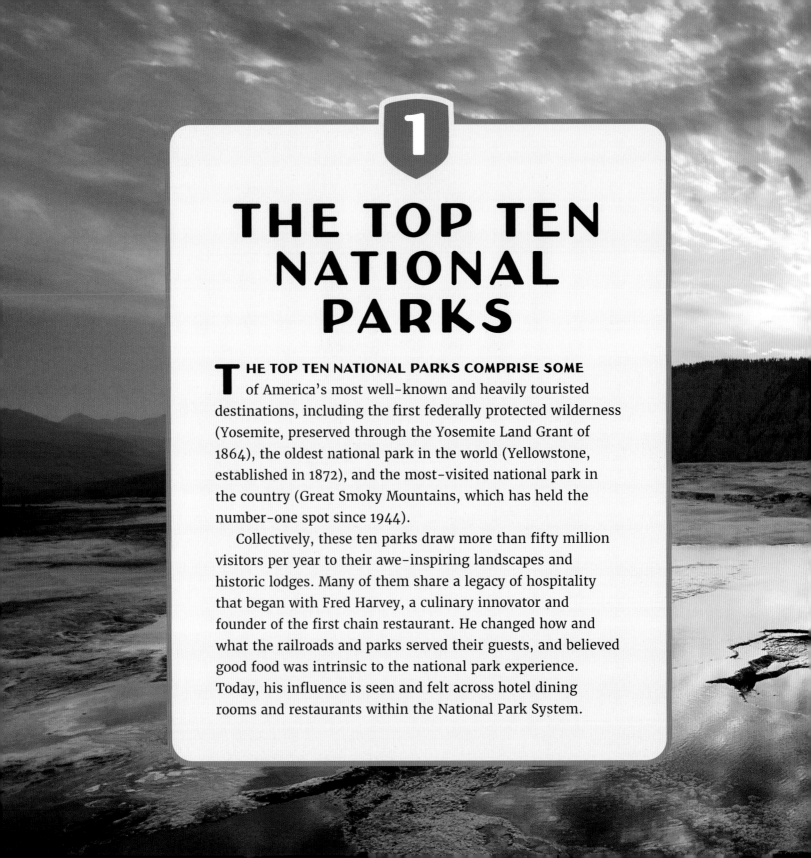

1

THE TOP TEN NATIONAL PARKS

THE TOP TEN NATIONAL PARKS COMPRISE SOME of America's most well-known and heavily touristed destinations, including the first federally protected wilderness (Yosemite, preserved through the Yosemite Land Grant of 1864), the oldest national park in the world (Yellowstone, established in 1872), and the most-visited national park in the country (Great Smoky Mountains, which has held the number-one spot since 1944).

Collectively, these ten parks draw more than fifty million visitors per year to their awe-inspiring landscapes and historic lodges. Many of them share a legacy of hospitality that began with Fred Harvey, a culinary innovator and founder of the first chain restaurant. He changed how and what the railroads and parks served their guests, and believed good food was intrinsic to the national park experience. Today, his influence is seen and felt across hotel dining rooms and restaurants within the National Park System.

Yellowstone National Park

Olympic National Park

1

BLACKBERRY LAVENDER JAM

Before the Great Smoky Mountains were established as a national park in 1934, thousands of families lived and farmed on the land. In addition to hunting, growing food, and pasturing livestock, these early European settlers roamed the hillsides every summer in search of nature's bounty: edible flowers, fresh wild berries, and medicinal herbs. They filled their buckets with all kinds of foraged foods and brought them back to their homesteads to preserve for the winter ahead.

This old-fashioned, small-batch fruit jam is an homage to that pioneering spirit—and it's the next best thing to picking ripe summer berries right off the trail on Andrews Bald.

MAKES TWO HALF-PINT (240 ML) JARS

1 pound (454 g) blackberries

¾ cup (150 g) sugar

2 large lavender sprigs (leaves and blossoms)

INSTRUCTIONS

Place a small plate in the freezer to chill until needed.

In a medium-size saucepan, combine the blackberries and sugar. Crush the blackberries with a potato masher until they release some juice, then add the lavender sprigs and bring the mixture to a full boil over medium-high to high heat, stirring occasionally.

Reduce the heat to maintain a vigorous simmer and cook for about 10 minutes, stirring frequently to prevent burning, until the mixture thickens and the jam reaches the gel stage. To test for gelling, drop a spoonful of the boiling mixture onto the chilled plate and put it in the freezer for 1 minute to cool completely. Remove the plate and use your fingertip to push against the side of the mixture. A properly set gel will "wrinkle" when it's pushed. If it's still a little runny, simmer the jam for 5 minutes more and test again.

Remove the jam from the heat and discard the lavender sprigs. Transfer the jam into clean jars, seal with a lid, and refrigerate for up to 3 months.

GREAT SMOKY MOUNTAINS NATIONAL PARK

BLACKBERRY OAT CRUMBLE

Blackberries start ripening in the Great Smoky Mountains when the days are long and the air is warm, beginning in the lower elevations and working their way up the hillsides. Going on nature walks and foraging for wild food is a favorite activity in the park, but visitors are sometimes surprised to see they aren't the only ones searching for sweet, juicy berries—the bears love them, too!

Berries grow abundantly in the Smokies, serving as the staple summer diet for black bears—and as trail snacks for hikers—and they're the inspiration for this blackberry oat crumble, a simple pastry that can double as breakfast or dessert.

MAKES SIXTEEN BARS

INGREDIENTS

Nonstick cooking spray

2 heaping cups (300 g) fresh blackberries

1 tablespoon (12.5 g) sugar

1 tablespoon (8 g) cornstarch

1 ½ cups (180 g) all-purpose flour

1 ½ cups (120 g) quick-cooking oats

1 cup (225 g) packed brown sugar

⅓ cup (37 g) chopped pecans

½ teaspoon baking soda

½ teaspoon kosher salt

¼ teaspoon ground nutmeg

1 cup (2 sticks, or 224 g) butter, at room temperature

INSTRUCTIONS

Preheat the oven to 350°F (180°C or gas mark 4).

Line a 9 × 9-inch (23 × 23 cm) baking dish with parchment paper and coat it with a thin film of cooking spray.

In a small bowl, combine the blackberries, sugar, and cornstarch. Set aside.

In the bowl of a stand mixer fitted with a paddle attachment, or in a large bowl and using a handheld electric mixer, beat the flour, oats, brown sugar, pecans, baking soda, salt, and nutmeg until combined. Add the butter and beat on low speed until the mixture resembles coarse crumbs.

Spread half the oat mixture evenly across the prepared baking dish. Press the mixture firmly into the bottom of the dish. Spread the blackberry mixture evenly over the oats. Sprinkle the remaining oat mixture over the blackberries, but do not press down.

Bake for 30 to 35 minutes until golden brown. Let cool completely, then slice into sixteen squares.

GREAT SMOKY MOUNTAINS NATIONAL PARK

FRENCH ONION SOUP GRATINÉE

Perched on the precipitous edge of the Grand Canyon, El Tovar (a National Historic Landmark) hails from the days of the Santa Fe Railway. When it was completed in 1905 (seven years before Arizona gained statehood and fourteen years before the establishment of the national park), it was considered the most elegant hotel west of the Mississippi with a first-class dining room to match. At one time, the hotel even had its own greenhouses for growing fruits and vegetables, a private herd of cows with a milking barn, a poultry farm, a butcher shop, and a bakery.

Some things change, of course, but some things don't: Their signature French onion soup has been a mainstay on the menu for decades. El Tovar hasn't shared their recipe, but I think this one is pretty close! So, turn on the music, pour yourself a glass of the wine you'll be using, and spend some quality time near the stove to make this mouthwatering classic—the key to a richly flavored French onion soup is not to rush the process.

MAKES EIGHT SERVINGS

INGREDIENTS

2 tablespoons (14 g) butter

¼ cup (60 ml) olive oil

5 pounds (2.3 kg) onions, thinly sliced

¼ cup (30 g) all-purpose flour

4 garlic cloves, minced

¼ cup (60 ml) sherry wine

½ cup (120 ml) dry red wine

½ cup (120 ml) dry white wine

8 cups (1.9 L) beef stock

5 thyme sprigs

2 bay leaves

Salt and ground black pepper

1 French baguette, cut into 1-inch (2.5 cm)-thick slices

Olive oil for drizzling

Grated Gruyère cheese for serving

INSTRUCTIONS

In a large, heavy-bottom pot over medium heat, melt the butter in the oil. Add the onions and stir to coat. Cover the pot and cook for 15 to 20 minutes until the onions have softened and released their liquid. Remove the lid and continue cooking until the onions are deep brown in color and reduced to half their volume, stirring occasionally and scraping the bottom of the pot to prevent sticking and burning. Full caramelization may take up to 1 hour.

recipe continues

GRAND CANYON NATIONAL PARK

Once the onions are caramelized, increase the heat to high. Stir in the flour and garlic and cook for 1 minute. Pour in the sherry, red wine, and white wine and cook until the liquid has evaporated, scraping up all the browned bits from the bottom of the pot. Add the stock, thyme, and bay leaves and bring the soup to a simmer. Cover and lower the heat to maintain a simmer. Cook for about 30 minutes.

Meanwhile, preheat the oven to 400°F (200°C or gas mark 6).

Arrange the baguette slices on a large sheet pan and drizzle with oil. Bake for 6 to 8 minutes until toasted and golden brown around the edges. Set aside.

Taste the soup and season with salt and pepper, as needed. Discard the thyme and bay leaves. Ladle the soup into ovenproof bowls, filling them about three-quarters full. Top each bowl with one or two toasted baguette slices and a generous amount of cheese.

Place an oven rack 6 to 8 inches (15 to 20 cm) from the heat and switch the oven to the broiler. Arrange the bowls on a sheet pan and broil for 2 to 4 minutes until the cheese is bubbling and slightly browned.

RECIPE NOTE

I don't specify any particular variety of onions in this recipe because they're all good, and each adds a slightly different dimension to the soup. Personally, I like to use a mix (red, yellow, and sweet) for a more layered, complex flavor.

AT-HOME TIP

Ideally, you should use a pot that's wider than it is tall (like a Dutch oven), but if all you have is a deep stockpot with tall sides, it will take longer to caramelize the onions because they won't have as much surface area for browning. If you don't have ovenproof bowls for serving, sprinkle a generous amount of cheese on the baguette slices before toasting. Then, top each soup bowl with a cheesy crouton to serve.

THREE SISTERS CHILI

Before there was a national park, the Grand Canyon was (and still is) a sacred land to Native American tribes that have lived in and around the canyon for centuries. These tribes work with the National Park Service to preserve their legacy and heritage within the park, and you can't miss the strong Native American influence throughout the canyon's place names and architecture. This influence even extends to the menu at Bright Angel Lodge, where a bowl of Three Sisters Chili honors the three most important agricultural crops of Indigenous farmers: beans, corn, and squash. According to Native American legend, these crops were inseparable sisters—gifts from the Great Spirit—and should be planted together, eaten together, and celebrated together.

Inspired by these ingredients, I created my own Three Sisters Chili, which can easily be made vegetarian by substituting vegetable broth.

MAKES EIGHT SERVINGS

INGREDIENTS

2 tablespoons (30 ml) olive oil

1 yellow onion, diced

2 poblano peppers, finely diced (see Recipe Note)

1 Anaheim pepper, finely diced

6 garlic cloves, minced

2 pounds (908 g) cubed butternut squash (1/2- to 1-inch, or 1 to 2.5 cm, cubes)

4 cups (960 ml) chicken broth, divided

1 (28-ounce, or 794 g) can diced fire-roasted tomatoes

2 cups (310 g) sweet corn kernels

1 (15-ounce, or 425 g) can kidney beans, rinsed and drained

1 (15-ounce, or 425 g) can black beans, rinsed and drained

2 teaspoons ground cumin

2 teaspoons ground coriander

2 teaspoons kosher salt

1 teaspoon dried oregano

1/2 teaspoon ground black pepper

1 bay leaf

1/2 cup chopped fresh cilantro

Sour cream or créme fraîche for garnishing (optional)

INSTRUCTIONS

Place a Dutch oven over medium-high heat and drizzle in the oil. Add the onion, poblanos, and Anaheim pepper and cook for about 5 minutes, stirring occasionally, until the onion is soft and translucent. Add the garlic and cook for 1 minute. Add the butternut squash, 3 cups (720 ml) of broth, the tomatoes, corn, kidney beans, black beans, cumin, coriander, salt, oregano, pepper, and bay leaf and bring to a boil. Cover the pot, reduce the heat to maintain a simmer, and cook for about 20 minutes, stirring occasionally. If the chili is too thick, add the remaining broth, 1/2 cup (120 ml) at a time, until the consistency is to your liking. (You might not need it all.)

Remove the cover, stir in the cilantro, and cook for 5 minutes until the squash is fork-tender and the mixture has slightly thickened. Taste the chili and season with more salt and pepper, if desired. Discard the bay leaf.

Serve each bowl with a dollop of sour cream (if using).

recipe continues

GRAND CANYON NATIONAL PARK

RECIPE NOTE

In grocery stores, poblano peppers are often mislabeled as pasilla peppers (which are actually the dried form of chilaca chile peppers). What you want are large, fresh peppers with a wide shape and dark green color.

HIKER'S STEW

Nestled nearly 4,600 feet (1.4 km) below the rim of the Grand Canyon, Phantom Ranch (a historic bunkhouse and restaurant dating back to 1922) can only be reached on foot, by mule, or by rafting the Colorado River. It's a popular stopover for hikers and mule riders who come for a cold drink and some hot stew after a strenuous trek to the bottom of the canyon.

The famous Hiker's Stew has been served at Phantom Ranch since the early 1970s. The original recipe served forty-four people and used canned vegetables, but mine is scaled for a family and uses fresh ingredients—a nice advantage when you don't need pack mules to bring all your groceries to you.

MAKES SIX SERVINGS

INGREDIENTS

2 pounds (908g) cubed stew beef

1 onion, diced

2 celery stalks, diced

2 cups (480 ml) beef broth

2 cups (480 ml) water

1/2 cup (120 ml) Burgundy wine

1/2 cup (120 ml) red wine vinegar

2 teaspoons dried thyme

2 teaspoons dried oregano

1 teaspoon garlic powder

1/2 teaspoon ground black pepper

1/2 teaspoon ground cloves

1 bay leaf

1 pound (454 g) Yukon Gold potatoes, cut into 1/2- to 1-inch (1 to 2.5 cm) chunks

2 cups (200 g) cut (1-inch, or 2.5 cm, pieces) green beans

2 cups (260 g) diced carrots

2 cups (310 g) corn kernels

2 tablespoons (160 g) cornstarch

2 tablespoons (30 ml) cold water

INSTRUCTIONS

In a medium-size stockpot over medium heat, cook the stew beef until all the liquid boils off and a dark scum forms, stirring occasionally. (Be patient, as this dark scum is the secret to the stew's signature flavor!) Add the onion, celery, broth, water, wine, vinegar, thyme, oregano, garlic powder, pepper, cloves, and bay leaf. Bring to a simmer, then cover and cook for 3 to 4 hours until the beef is very tender, reducing the heat, as needed, to maintain a low, gentle simmer.

Add the potatoes, green beans, carrots, and corn and bring the stew to a boil. Reduce the heat to maintain a simmer and cook for 30 minutes until the vegetables are tender, stirring occasionally. Discard the bay leaf.

In a small bowl, make a slurry by whisking the cornstarch and cold water until smooth. Gradually whisk the slurry into the stew and simmer for 5 minutes, then turn off the heat. Cover and keep warm until ready to serve.

GRAND CANYON
NATIONAL PARK

GRAND CANYON MULES

Mules were once used for mining operations in the Grand Canyon until it became more profitable to use them for transporting tourists to the canyon floor. Since the late 1800s, mules have carried more than a million people in and out of the canyon! The sturdy and steadfast animals are a familiar and beloved sight on the trails, and even have a drink named after them: the Grand Canyon Mule. El Tovar and Fred Harvey Tavern offer a few fun twists on the classic Moscow Mule, but these are my favorites, re-created from the originals.

Grand Canyon Mule

MAKES ONE SERVING

INGREDIENTS

½ lime, cut into 2 wedges

2 ounces (60 ml) vodka

½ cup (120 ml) ginger beer

1 mint sprig

Lime wheel for garnishing

INSTRUCTIONS

Squeeze the lime wedges into a chilled copper mug and drop in the spent shells. Add ice, then pour in the vodka and top with ginger beer. Stir to combine and garnish with the mint sprig and a lime wheel.

Shriveled Apple Mule

MAKES ONE SERVING

INGREDIENTS

½ lime, cut into 2 wedges

2 ounces (60 ml) Jack Daniel's Tennessee apple whiskey

2 ounces (60 ml) Martinelli's apple cider

⅓ cup (80 ml) ginger beer

Apple slice for garnishing

Lime wheel for garnishing

INSTRUCTIONS

Squeeze the lime wedges into a chilled copper mug and drop in the spent shells. Add ice, then pour in the whiskey and cider and top with ginger beer. Stir to combine and garnish with an apple slice and a lime wheel.

Indian Garden Mule

MAKES ONE SERVING

INGREDIENTS

½ lemon, halved

1 ounce (30 ml) cucumber vodka

1 ounce (30 ml) blueberry vodka

½ cup (120 ml) ginger beer

Blueberries for garnishing

1 mint sprig

Lemon wheel for garnishing

INSTRUCTIONS

Squeeze the lemon halves into a chilled copper mug and drop in the spent shells. Add ice, then pour in the cucumber vodka and blueberry vodka and top with ginger beer. Stir to combine and garnish with a spoonful of blueberries, a mint sprig, and a lemon wheel.

GRAND CANYON NATIONAL PARK

THE FRED HARVEY LEGACY

Before passenger train dining cars were common amenities, rail passengers in the late nineteenth century had few options for eating in transit: They could buy overpriced sandwiches on the train platform to take to their hard wooden seats in overcrowded coaches, or they could sit down at a roadhouse for stale coffee, cold beans, rancid meat, and greasy stew—all served with a surly or otherwise indifferent attitude. It's no wonder, then, that the simple lack of a decent meal discouraged many Americans from traveling westward to visit places like the Grand Canyon and Yellowstone.

Fred Harvey, an English-born immigrant, experienced such indignities while working for the railroads and traveling frequently by train. Appalled at the indigestible fare and poor service he received at train stations and depot hotels, the former restaurant owner turned freight agent convinced the Atchison, Topeka, and Santa Fe Railway (then the smallest of the competing lines) that he could do better. They closed the deal on a handshake and Harvey took over the dingy dining room at the Topeka, Kansas, train depot, importing fine china, linens, silverware, and stemware for his venture.

The first Harvey House was born in 1876—and it was an instant success. (It certainly helped that the railway provided him free space and utilities, allowing Harvey to keep all the profits.)

Harvey then opened a second trackside restaurant in Florence, Kansas, elevating his guests' dining experience by recruiting a famous chef from Chicago. The entrepreneur also devised an ingenious telegraph system to notify his restaurants, well in advance of train arrivals, of what people would be eating, making it possible to feed hundreds of passengers in just thirty minutes (the allotted time for trains to stop and refuel).

Revolutionary for its time, good food served promptly was the hallmark of the Harvey House experience. In sharp contrast to many other Western eateries, Harvey Houses offered the freshest ingredients (delivered daily from refrigerated railroad cars straight to their kitchens, thanks to Harvey's partnership with AT&SF) and clean, civilized rest stops for weary travelers. Soon, Harvey Houses populated the Santa Fe line, and as tourism increased, Harvey added dozens more restaurants, bookstores, gift shops, hotels, and newsstands throughout the West.

But Harvey didn't stop at merely erecting more buildings. After several brawls broke out between his customers and his African American waiters in Raton, New Mexico (the wildest part of the Wild

West), he made a radical change. He decided to employ the nation's first all-female workforce, putting ads in newspapers seeking single, hardworking, well-mannered, and intelligent white women between the ages of eighteen and thirty.

Women lacked opportunities for independence in the late 1800s, and working women were looked down upon for shirking their wifely and motherly responsibilities. Harvey gave women an "out" while fostering a pleasant, professional environment for his patrons and waitstaff. Requirements were strict: The women had a curfew, could not wear makeup or jewelry, dressed in demure uniforms, and lived together in dormitories overseen by a "house mother."

Despite the rigorous standards, thousands of women from the Midwest and the East saw waitressing for Harvey as a way to earn a respectable living and make a new life in the adventurous West. A Harvey House waitress earned $17.50 per month plus room, board, and tips—a generous income by the standards of the time. In the early twentieth century, waitresses were considered lower class, but the "Harvey Girls," as his waitresses were called, brought elegance and decorum to the Wild West and became a signature component of his success. Some even say the Harvey Girls helped populate the region, as many went on to marry railway workers, ranchers, or local townspeople, and many a baby in the day was christened Fred or Harvey in honor of their origins.

So, Harvey—who not only created the first national chain of quality restaurants, the first national chain of resort hotels, and the first national chain of retail stores (the first national chain of anything, really)—also created the first matchmaking service of sorts. (Kidding, but not.)

Harvey established standards for hospitality and is credited with teaching much of America how to eat well, as the food in his restaurants and hotels was as good as (if not better than) any fine establishment in Chicago, New York, or Paris.

His company's crowning achievement—that he did not live to see—was the construction of El Tovar, a four-star hotel at the lip of the Grand Canyon.

In 1901, AT&SF completed the new branch line to the Grand Canyon so a Harvey House hotel could be built there. (The Union Pacific Railroad had a branch line to Yellowstone, and AT&SF wanted their own natural wonder to attract tourists.)

When Harvey died that same year, his son Ford took over the planning and design of a grand tourist lodge that stood just 330 feet (100.5 m) from the new AT&SF train depot. The company spared no expense in building the lodge. When El Tovar opened in 1905, it redefined tourism in the Southwest by offering luxurious accommodations, providing New York–quality food and service in the middle of nowhere, and introducing the world to Native American art, cowboy culture, and mission architecture.

Today, El Tovar retains much of its eclectic nineteenth-century character as well as its famed dining room. It's also one of the few Harvey Houses still in existence (another one being the Bright Angel Lodge on the South Rim of the Grand Canyon). Though the Fred Harvey Company no longer owns the hotels, Harvey's legacy lives on by continuing to set the standard for lodging, dining, and concessions in the National Park System as well as the rest of America.

BOURBON ELK CHILI

Rocky Mountain National Park is best known for two things: imposing mountains (the park is one of the country's highest national parks, with elevations topping fourteen thousand feet, or 4.25 km) and elk (which are among the largest, loudest, and most abundant wild animals in the park). Though they're a common sight these days, at one time the elk population in the state was nearly wiped out by hunting and human encroachment. Elk were reintroduced in the early 1900s by relocating a small herd from Wyoming to Colorado.

Through decades of conservation efforts, Colorado now boasts the largest elk population in the world. You don't have to be a hunter to get your hands on wild game, however; elk meat is readily available throughout the Rockies and across the northern United States.

MAKES SIX SERVINGS

INGREDIENTS

2 pounds (908 g) ground elk

2 tablespoons (30 ml) olive oil

2 bell peppers, any color, diced

1 yellow onion, diced

½ cup (120 ml) freshly squeezed orange juice

1 (28-ounce, or 794 g) can crushed tomatoes

1 (15-ounce, or 425 g) can tomato sauce

1 (12-ounce, or 360 ml) can dark beer (such as a stout or brown ale), plus more as needed

3 canned chipotle peppers in adobo sauce, minced

2 tablespoons (15 g) ancho chile powder

1 tablespoon (5 g) unsweetened cocoa powder

2 teaspoons kosher salt, plus more to taste

2 teaspoons smoked paprika

2 teaspoons ground cumin

1 teaspoon ground coriander

¼ teaspoon cayenne pepper

1 (14-ounce, or 395 g) can kidney beans, rinsed and drained

1 (14-ounce, or 395 g) can black beans, rinsed and drained

½ cup (120 ml) bourbon

SUGGESTED ACCOMPANIMENTS

Shredded cheddar cheese

Sliced scallions

Sliced jalapeño peppers

Tortilla chips

Sour cream

INSTRUCTIONS

In a Dutch oven over medium-high heat, cook the ground elk for 6 to 8 minutes, or just until browned, stirring to break up the meat. Add the oil, bell peppers, and onion and cook for about 5 minutes until tender, stirring occasionally. Pour in the orange juice and scrape up any browned bits, then add the crushed tomatoes, tomato sauce, beer, chipotles, and all the spices and bring to a simmer. Partially cover the pot and cook for about 30 minutes, stirring occasionally and reducing the heat, as needed, to maintain a simmer.

Stir in the kidney beans and black beans, return the chili to a simmer, and cook, uncovered, for about 30 minutes. If the mixture looks too thick, add more beer until the consistency is to your liking. Taste and add more salt, as needed.

Stir in the bourbon just before serving and top each bowl with your favorite accompaniments.

ROCKY MOUNTAIN NATIONAL PARK

RED CURRANT CAIPIRINHA

From spring to fall, wax currants blanket the Rockies in a strong spicy scent, wafting from the low foothills to the high mountain slopes. The scrubby bushes are flush with edible red berries in late summer that provide an energizing snack on the trail for hikers and backpackers. These currants are the inspiration for my caipirinha-with-a-twist, which infuses the classic Brazilian cocktail with the juicy tartness of red currants (a more commonly available cousin of wax currants).

INSTRUCTIONS

Slice off the white and fibrous inner portion of each lime quarter (the pith) to reduce bitterness. (This is the secret to a true caipirinha.) Then, cut each lime quarter in half crosswise for a total of eight wedges. Muddle the lime wedges, currants, and sugar in a rocks glass. Pour in the cachaça and lime juice and stir gently until the sugar is mostly dissolved. Top with ice before serving.

=== MAKES ONE SERVING ===

INGREDIENTS

1 lime, quartered lengthwise

⅓ cup (56 g) red currants

2 tablespoons (25 g) sugar

2 ounces (60 ml) cachaça

2 tablespoons (30 ml) freshly squeezed lime juice

ROCKY MOUNTAIN NATIONAL PARK

NAVAJO TACOS

Navajo tacos are a unique staple of many restaurants and roadside stands throughout the Four Corners, but their invention was relatively recent. They were created by Lou Shepard, who worked for the tribe as manager of the now-defunct Navajo Lodge in Window Rock, Arizona. In 1964, a hungry guest inspired him to pull together a mishmash meal using whatever he could find in the kitchen: fry bread, some beans, chile peppers, and a tossed salad. After the guest raved about his concoction, Lou put the new item on his menu and "Lou's Special" became an instant hit with travelers and Natives alike.

The term "Navajo tacos" stuck after a customer ordered it by that name, and in the decades since, they've been adapted and served all over the Southwest and even outside the Navajo Nation, where they're known simply as Indian tacos.

The Red Rock Grill in Zion serves their version with beef chili, but I've put my own spin on it with a homemade shortcut chili—you can even use canned chili. Either way, you can't go wrong with these open-face tacos.

━━━ MAKES SIX SERVINGS ━━━

INGREDIENTS

FOR CHILI

2 tablespoons (30 ml) olive oil

1 yellow onion, diced

1 pound (454 g) lean ground beef

2 tablespoons (15 g) chili powder, plus more as needed

1 tablespoon (7 g) ground cumin, plus more as needed

1 teaspoon kosher salt, plus more to taste

½ teaspoon ground black pepper, plus more to taste

1 (28-ounce, or 794 g) can diced tomatoes, drained

1 (15-ounce, or 425 g) can kidney beans, rinsed and drained

1½ cups (390 g) salsa (use your favorite brand)

½ cup (8 g) chopped fresh cilantro

FOR TACOS

12 Navajo Fry Breads (page 111)

2 cups (85 g) shredded lettuce

2 cups (360 g) diced Roma tomatoes

1 cup (160 g) diced red onion

1 cup (115 g) shredded Monterey Jack cheese

1 cup (115 g) shredded cheddar cheese

Sour cream for serving

Salsa for serving

Guacamole for serving

INSTRUCTIONS

To make the chili: Place a large saucepan over medium-high heat and drizzle in the oil. Add the onion and cook for 2 to 3 minutes until soft and translucent. Add the ground beef, sprinkle it with the chili powder, cumin, salt, and pepper and cook for 5 to 7 minutes until browned, stirring frequently to break apart the meat.

Stir in the tomatoes, kidney beans, and salsa and simmer for 30 to 40 minutes until the mixture is reduced to a chili-like consistency, reducing the heat, as needed, to maintain a simmer. If the chili is too thick, add a little water. Adjust the seasonings to your preference as it cooks. Once the chili is done, stir in the cilantro.

To make the tacos: Arrange the fry bread on plates and top each with a few spoonfuls of chili, lettuce, tomato, red onion, Monterey Jack, and cheddar. (Save any leftover chili to eat later.) Serve with sour cream, salsa, and guacamole on the side.

recipe continues

ZION
NATIONAL PARK

DID YOU KNOW

Fry bread is the official state bread of South Dakota, so it's no surprise you can find Indian tacos at Badlands National Park as well. At Cedar Pass Lodge, they serve Sioux Indian tacos, which feature bison meat instead of beef.

BOYSENBERRY PIE

Located in the center of the jaw-dropping Yosemite Valley near iconic landmarks like Half Dome and Glacier Point, The Ahwahnee is a landmark itself. Built in 1927 and designated as a National Historic Landmark, the hotel has hosted an impressive roster of guests (including U.S. presidents, British royalty, and Hollywood celebrities) and boasts a grand dining room that's famed for its food as well as its architecture.

Even after many renovations and a brief name change for the hotel, one thing has remained constant: this boysenberry pie, which has been on the menu for more than sixty years. Served with a scoop of vanilla ice cream, it makes the perfect summer dessert.

MAKES EIGHT SERVINGS

INGREDIENTS

FOR PIE FILLING

1½ cups (198 g) frozen boysenberries

¾ cup (150 g) sugar

1¼ ounces (35 g) clear instant gelatin

Pinch of salt

FOR CRUST

9 ounces (255 g) all-purpose flour, plus more for dusting

4½ ounces (130 g) butter, at room temperature

1½ tablespoons (18.75 g) sugar

Pinch of salt

1½ ounces (45 ml) very cold water

1 egg, lightly beaten with 1 tablespoon (15 ml) water to make an egg wash

INSTRUCTIONS

To make the pie filling: In a medium-size saucepan over low heat, slowly cook the boysenberries for 5 minutes, stirring occasionally.

In a small bowl, stir together the sugar, gelatin, and salt. Add the sugar mixture to the berries and cook for 5 minutes, stirring frequently to avoid burning. Set aside to cool.

To make the crust: In a food processor, combine the flour, butter, sugar, and salt. Process until the ingredients are well blended, then add the cold water all at once. Turn off the food processor as soon as the dough binds and pulls away from the sides of the bowl. Roll the dough into a ball, wrap it tightly in plastic wrap, and refrigerate for 1 hour.

Preheat the oven to 350°F (180°C or gas mark 4).

Lightly dust a work surface with flour and place the dough on it. Use a rolling pin to roll the dough into a circle, ⅛ inch (0.3 cm) thick. Fit the dough into a 10-inch (25 cm) pie pan, getting it down into the corners. Trim the edge with kitchen shears so the dough overhangs the pan by ½ inch (1 cm) all around. Tuck the overhanging edge under itself all the way around the pie, then bake the crust for 5 minutes.

Meanwhile, reroll the dough scraps into another ⅛-inch (0.3 cm)-thick circle to form a top for the pie. Cover with a towel.

Remove the crust from the oven and fill it with the boysenberry mixture. Brush the egg wash along the edge of the bottom crust, place the top crust over it, then crimp the edges with your fingers to seal. Cut four slits on top for steam to vent, and brush more egg wash all over the top.

Bake for 15 to 20 minutes until golden brown. Let cool completely before serving.

YOSEMITE NATIONAL PARK

EL CAPITINI–THE FIRST ASCENT

Yosemite's signature cocktail is a nod to the groundbreaking 1958 first ascent of El Capitan, a stark granite monolith soaring over three thousand feet (0.9 km) into the sky. It took Warren Harding, Wayne Merry, and George Whitmore forty-seven days—over a course of eighteen months—to climb The Nose, now known as the most famous rock climbing route in North America. Why did it take so long to complete the climb?

Legend has it that Warren Harding was a notorious tippler. He consumed copious amounts of cheap red wine while suspended on a cliff ledge in his bivy and constantly sent someone in his party down to replenish his supply during the climb.

I'm sure Harding is raising a glass (or perhaps a Sierra cup) from up above, not only for his achievements but for having a drink named after his legacy. At The Ahwahnee, the celebratory climber's cocktail is served with a souvenir mini carabiner clipped to the glass.

MAKES ONE SERVING

INGREDIENTS

1 lemon wedge

Sugar for rimming glass

1 ounce (30 ml) vodka

½ ounce (15 ml) Cointreau

½ ounce (15 ml) PAMA pomegranate liqueur (not juice)

Splash of pineapple juice

Champagne for topping (Domaine Ste. Michelle Brut preferred)

Orange twist for garnishing

INSTRUCTIONS

Juice the lemon wedge and use the rind to wet the rim of a chilled martini glass. Pour the sugar onto a plate and gently press the wet rim of the glass into the sugar.

Fill a cocktail shaker with ice and pour in the vodka, Cointreau, PAMA, and pineapple juice. Cover and shake well, then strain the drink into the prepared martini glass. Top with a Champagne float and garnish with an orange twist. (Bonus points if you tie the orange twist into a climber's knot before serving.)

YOSEMITE NATIONAL PARK

FIREFALL

This chile-spiked winter cocktail, a specialty of The Ahwahnee Bar in Yosemite, is named for the "firefall" at Horsetail Fall, a small, seasonal waterfall that's easy to miss among the more impressive features in the park. But on certain weeks in February, if conditions are just right, the angle of the setting sun creates a dazzling illusion behind the fall that makes the water appear as a streaming ribbon of molten lava.

The natural phenomenon is reminiscent of the original firefall that started in the late nineteenth century. In those early days of Yosemite tourism, burning logs were pushed over Glacier Point every night, lighting the water in a blaze of orange while people gathered and sang. The tradition continued until 1968, when National Park Service Director George Hartzog finally ended it because it was at odds with the park's mission to help people appreciate Yosemite's natural beauty.

INGREDIENTS

FOR FIREFALL HOT CHOCOLATE MIX

2 cups (320 g) Nestlé hot cocoa mix

1 tablespoon (7.5 g) pasilla chile powder, plus more for sprinkling

1 tablespoon (7 g) ground cinnamon, plus more for sprinkling

FOR FIREFALL COCKTAIL

¾ ounce (22.5 ml) tequila (Sauza Gold preferred)

¾ ounce (22.5 ml) crème de cacao brown (DeKuyper preferred)

2 tablespoons (20 g) Firefall Hot Chocolate Mix

Boiling water for topping

Whipped cream for garnishing

INSTRUCTIONS

To make the Firefall hot chocolate mix: In a small bowl, stir together all the ingredients and set aside.

To make the Firefall cocktail: In an Irish coffee mug, combine the tequila and crème de cacao brown. Add the hot chocolate mix, then fill the glass with boiling water. Stir well. Top with whipped cream and sprinkle with chile powder and cinnamon to serve.

Store any leftover hot chocolate mix in an airtight container for future cocktails.

YOSEMITE
NATIONAL PARK

MOOSE DROOL-BRAISED BISON SHORT RIBS

No, there are no animal secretions in this dish. The legendary ribs are named for the local beer they're braised in all day, producing a fall-off-the-bone tenderness that has made this recipe a mainstay on the Old Faithful Snow Lodge menu for more than a decade. If you can't get your hands on Moose Drool, use any rich brown ale or amber ale for the sauce; the nuance of that beer will create a depth of flavor that makes your version of Yellowstone's signature bison short ribs deliciously unique. I recommend serving these with polenta, mashed potatoes, or roasted vegetables.

================ **MAKES EIGHT SERVINGS** ================

INGREDIENTS

½ cup (120 ml) vegetable oil

1 cup (120 g) all-purpose flour

1 tablespoon (15 g) kosher salt

2 teaspoons ground black pepper

10 pounds (4.5 kg) bone-in bison short ribs

2 yellow onions, diced

2 celery stalks, diced

4 carrots, diced

4 garlic cloves, minced

7 tablespoons (112 g) tomato paste

2 teaspoons chopped fresh thyme leaves

1 (12-ounce, or 360 ml) can Moose Drool Brown Ale or your favorite brown ale

3 cups (720 ml) beef broth

1 cup (240 ml) Burgundy wine

2 cups (480 g) demi-glace, prepared from mix (see Recipe Note)

Chopped fresh parsley for garnishing

INSTRUCTIONS

Preheat the oven to 275°F (140°C or gas mark 1).

In a large skillet over medium-high heat, heat the oil.

In a shallow dish, stir together the flour, salt, and pepper. Dip the short ribs in the seasoned flour, coating both sides evenly. Working in batches, sear both sides of the floured ribs in the skillet, cooking to a deep brown color. Do not sear too many ribs at once, or the skillet will cool and they won't brown properly. As the ribs are seared, remove them from the skillet and stand on end in a large roasting pan (at least 3 inches, or 7.5 cm, deep) for braising.

When the ribs are browned, remove excess oil from the skillet, leaving the fond (dark brown and black bits) from searing the ribs. Add the onions, celery, carrots, and garlic and cook for 6 to 8 minutes, stirring occasionally, until tender.

Stir in the tomato paste and thyme. Pour in the Moose Drool, broth, and wine to deglaze the skillet, scraping the bottom with a large spoon to incorporate the fond.

recipe continues

Pour the vegetables and liquid into the roasting pan containing the seared ribs, just enough to barely cover the ribs. (The meat will release more liquid as it cooks.) Cover the pan first with parchment paper, then aluminum foil and transfer to the oven. Braise for about 6 hours until the meat is fork-tender and pulling away from the bones.

Carefully remove the ribs from the braising liquid and keep warm. Stir in the prepared demi-glace to thicken the sauce slightly.

Serve the ribs with a generous drizzle of pan sauce and garnish with parsley. Use the leftover sauce to dress your side dishes.

RECIPE NOTE

The Yellowstone kitchen uses a demi-glace gravy mix to enrich their sauce, but any slightly thickened brown sauce will work—it's the Moose Drool that makes the flavors! You can use homemade demi-glace, demi-glace sauce mix, or powdered gravy mix; just follow the instructions on the package to prepare the needed amount.

TOMATO AND LAMB RAGOUT

It's no surprise that Yellowstone takes sustainability seriously. The world's first national park—established in 1872 to protect the land and local resources—strives to source as many ingredients as possible from nearby farms, ranches, fisheries, and brewers. In fact, more than half of the park's food purchases come from sustainable sources, and it uses Montana Natural Lamb (produced in Big Timber, Montana) for this popular ragout, which has appeared on a few menus throughout the park.

MAKES SIX SERVINGS

INGREDIENTS

2 tablespoons (30 ml) olive oil

1 yellow onion, diced

1 tablespoon (10 g) minced garlic

2 pounds (908 g) ground lamb

¼ cup (60 ml) Burgundy wine

3 (15-ounce, or 425 g) cans diced tomatoes

¼ cup (60 ml) Worcestershire sauce

3 tablespoons (7 g) chopped fresh thyme leaves

4 teaspoons (24 g) Better Than Bouillon beef soup base

1½ teaspoons kosher salt

1 teaspoon ground black pepper

⅓ cup (13 g) thinly sliced fresh basil

3 tablespoons (18 g) thinly sliced fresh mint

Cooked pasta for serving

Grated parmesan cheese for serving

INSTRUCTIONS

Place a Dutch oven over medium-high heat and drizzle in the oil. Add the onion and garlic and cook for 2 to 3 minutes until soft and translucent.

Add the ground lamb and cook for 5 to 7 minutes until browned, stirring frequently to break apart the meat. Pour in the wine and simmer for 10 minutes, stirring occasionally.

Add the tomatoes and their juices, Worcestershire sauce, thyme, soup base, salt, and pepper and bring to a low simmer; adjust the heat to maintain a simmer; and cook for 1 hour until the mixture is reduced to a thick sauce consistency.

Fold in the basil and mint and simmer for 5 minutes.

Serve the ragout with your favorite pasta, sprinkled with parmesan.

Pictured: Tomato and lamb ragout served with pappardelle.

YELLOWSTONE
NATIONAL PARK

ROOSEVELT BAKED BEANS

Most people visit national parks to get away, but people who stay at the Roosevelt Lodge in Yellowstone really do get away from it all. As the least crowded lodge in the least developed area of the park, it offers an outstanding Wild West experience with chuckwagon rides, horseback rides, and ample wildlife viewing in Lamar Valley.

These Roosevelt Baked Beans are one of the most requested recipes from the park, appearing on menus in the Roosevelt Lodge Dining Room as well as its scenic Old West Dinner Cookout.

MAKES SIX TO EIGHT SERVINGS

INGREDIENTS

8 ounces (225 g) bacon, chopped into ½-inch (1 cm) pieces

1 yellow onion, diced

1 pound (454 g) ground beef

1 (16-ounce, or 454 g) can pork and beans

1 (15-ounce, or 425 g) can kidney beans, rinsed and drained

1 (15-ounce, or 425 g) can lima beans, undrained

1 (15-ounce, or 425 g) can butter beans, undrained

½ cup (112.5 g) packed brown sugar

½ cup (120 g) ketchup

1 tablespoon (11 g) mustard

Salt and ground black pepper

INSTRUCTIONS

In a Dutch oven over medium-high heat, fry the bacon until crisp. Add the onion and cook for 2 to 3 minutes until soft and translucent.

Add the ground beef and cook for about 10 minutes until browned and cooked through, stirring with a large spoon to break apart the meat.

Add all the canned beans, brown sugar, ketchup, and mustard and stir to combine. Simmer for about 30 minutes to let the flavors develop, stirring periodically and adjusting the heat to maintain a simmer. Season with salt and pepper to taste.

AT-HOME TIP
For thicker beans, drain the liquid from the canned lima and butter beans before adding them to the pot.

YELLOWSTONE
NATIONAL PARK

HUCKLEBERRY COBBLER

At Yellowstone, anything made with huckleberries is an instant hit. The sweet-tart berries are harvested from the wild and turned into a number of desserts in the park's dining rooms, including the ever-popular huckleberry cobbler at Mammoth Hot Springs Hotel. Although guests are served the decadent dessert in individual ramekins, this at-home version (courtesy of former Executive Chef Mike Dean) can be made in a cast-iron skillet. My tip: Add a scoop of vanilla ice cream at the table!

——— MAKES EIGHT SERVINGS ———

INGREDIENTS

4 tablespoons (½ stick, or 56 g) butter, cut into small pieces

FOR FILLING

⅓ cup (67 g) granulated sugar

⅓ cup (75 g) brown sugar

3 tablespoons (24 g) cornstarch

½ teaspoon kosher salt

4 cups (600 g) fresh huckleberries

1 tablespoon (15 ml) freshly squeezed lemon juice

1 teaspoon vanilla extract

FOR BATTER

2 cups (240 g) all-purpose flour

1 cup (200 g) granulated sugar

1½ teaspoons baking soda

1 teaspoon kosher salt

4 eggs

1 cup (240 ml) milk

FOR STREUSEL TOPPING

1 cup (120 g) all-purpose flour

½ cup (112.5 g) brown sugar

8 tablespoons (1 stick, or 112 g) butter, at room temperature, cut into small pieces

INSTRUCTIONS

Preheat the oven to 375°F (190°C or gas mark 5). Scatter the butter in a 10-inch (25 cm) cast-iron skillet and place the skillet in the oven to melt while it preheats.

To make the filling: In a large bowl, stir together the granulated sugar, brown sugar, cornstarch, and salt. Add the huckleberries, lemon juice, and vanilla and toss to coat thoroughly.

To make the batter: In another large bowl, whisk the flour, granulated sugar, baking soda, and salt to blend. Add the eggs and milk and whisk into a smooth batter.

To make the streusel topping: In a small bowl, combine the flour and brown sugar. Cut the butter into the mixture with a fork until crumbles form and no dry flour remains.

Remove the hot skillet from the oven. Spread the filling across the hot skillet and pour the batter on top. Drop the streusel evenly over the batter, gently breaking up any crumbles that are too large, or squeezing small sandy bits together to form larger crumbles.

Place the skillet on a sheet pan to catch any overspills, then bake for 25 to 30 minutes until the fruit is bubbling and the cake is golden brown. Let stand for 10 minutes before serving.

YELLOWSTONE
NATIONAL PARK

BEST TRAIL SNACKS
(BASED ON YOUR FAVORITE NATIONAL PARK)

Does your favorite national park have a (subconscious) say in what you like to eat? Here's a fun "quiz" to find out: Pick your favorite national park and I'll tell you what kind of trail snacks match your personality!

If your favorite national park is . . .

CAPITOL REEF
The historic orchards at Capitol Reef contain about 1,900 fruit and nut trees—relics of the area's pioneer history. You're probably a fan of variety, so look to the original homesteaders for inspiration and jazz up your trail mix with dried apple chips, dried apricots, dried cherries, dried peach rings, almonds, pecans, and walnuts.

CUYAHOGA VALLEY
The Countryside Initiative began in 1999 as a way to preserve and protect the rural character and agricultural resources in Cuyahoga Valley. To date, the program has restored more than a dozen working farmsteads within the park, including egg producers. In support of local farms, why not enjoy a couple of pastured hard-boiled eggs as your trail snack?

DEATH VALLEY
Date palms dot the oases in Death Valley, softening an otherwise harsh and desolate landscape. Naturally, you can't get enough dates. The sweet, sticky fruits are delicious on their own, but you can also add Medjools, Deglet Noors, or deep purple Dayris to your homemade trail mix, granola, or energy balls.

GREAT BASIN
You go to Great Basin for solitude, starry night skies, and the sweet smell of nature. If you love the intoxicating fragrance of the park's pinyon pines that reminds you of fresh morning air in the desert, you'll want to fill your pack with pine nuts (and you actually can, see page 187). A handful can give you the energy boost you need on the trail.

GREAT SMOKY MOUNTAINS
You're drawn to the famous smoky haze that gives the Great Smoky Mountains their name—and their dreamy quality—but did you know the "smoke" is actually fog that comes from the area's vegetation? Regardless, I bet you'd like some smoky treats to hit the trail with, like smoked candied pecans, a Southern favorite.

HAWAII VOLCANOES
If you love the vibes—and the food—of Hawaii, spread the aloha with a tropical-themed trail mix to share with fellow hikers. Try dried tropical fruits, like pineapple, papaya, mango, and banana chips; macadamia nuts; and cacao nibs, all of which are grown on the Islands.

LAKE CLARK

Renowned for fishing, the pristine waters around Lake Clark are an angler's dream. Fuel up with some ready-to-eat wild Alaskan king salmon pouches—all you need is a fork and some crackers for a satisfying hit of salt and protein.

PINNACLES

Located just a hop from rolling vineyard-covered hills, a day at Pinnacles often ends with a jaunt through the local wine-tasting rooms. Raisins are right up your alley, giving you a burst of energy just when you need it. Mix the standard variety with golden raisins and flame raisins for added depth of flavor.

ROCKY MOUNTAIN

Elk abounds in the Rockies, and when you feel your stomach rumbling while you're out hiking and hoping to spot wildlife, reach for a handful of elk jerky. These snack sticks have a very mild game flavor and pack the perfect punch of protein on the go.

YELLOWSTONE

No doubt you've seen all the free-ranging bison herds on your visits to Yellowstone. But have you tried bison jerky? It's similar to beef, though it has a coarser texture and slightly sweeter flavor—and none of the gaminess you might expect. Pack a few strips for a healthy protein boost on your hike.

LOBSTER STEW

Acadia has the distinction of being the first national park east of the Mississippi, established in 1919 as Lafayette National Park and renamed in 1929 as Acadia National Park. But before there was a park, there was the Jordan Pond House, a historic restaurant on the southern end of Jordan Pond with a long tradition of serving their famous fluffy popovers (see Perfect Popovers for my version, page 63) and Gulf of Maine lobsters.

The lobster stew is an enduring favorite on the menu, and this version is adapted from their official recipe. Serve it with popovers and jam, just like they do at Jordan Pond—and don't be afraid of leftovers (if there are any!). This stew is even better when made the night before and reheated the following day.

===== **MAKES SIX SERVINGS** =====

INGREDIENTS

2 large lobsters (about 4 pounds, or 1.8 kg, total), steamed, meat freshly picked

4 tablespoons (½ stick, or 56 g) butter

1 tablespoon (8.4 g) paprika

1 cup (240 ml) sherry wine

4 cups (960 ml) milk

2 cups (480 ml) heavy cream

1 tablespoon (18 g) Better Than Bouillon lobster base

Salt and ground black pepper

Chopped fresh chives for garnishing

INSTRUCTIONS

Chop the lobster meat into bite-size pieces. You should have about 4 cups (580 g).

In a large skillet over medium heat, melt the butter. Add the lobster meat, sprinkle with paprika, and cook for about 5 minutes until warmed through, stirring to coat the lobster evenly with the butter. Pour in the sherry and bring to a simmer for 3 to 5 minutes, then remove from the heat.

In a large saucepan over medium-high heat, combine the milk and heavy cream and heat until the edges start to bubble, being careful not to boil the mixture. Stir the lobster base into the hot milk mixture. Add the lobster meat with its pan sauce and cook for 5 minutes to allow the flavors to blend. Season with salt and pepper to taste.

Ladle into bowls and serve with a sprinkle of chives on top.

ACADIA NATIONAL PARK

PERFECT POPOVERS

The famed Jordan Pond House served their first popovers in 1895. When the restaurant opened, the original proprietors, Thomas and Nellie McIntire, decided to start a tradition of luncheon, tea, and popovers on the lawn overlooking Jordan Pond and the mountains of Acadia. They continued to run the restaurant and host afternoon tea for the next fifty years until their retirement. Today, the Jordan Pond House bakes upwards of six thousand popovers a day—their biggest-selling menu item—for hungry guests all summer long.

Popovers can be tricky to master, and many copy-cat recipes try to replicate the Jordan Pond delicacies. Oftentimes, these attempts end in frustration as the popovers deflate (or never rise at all), so I've created my own recipe that works *every time*, even at altitude.

=== MAKES SIX POPOVERS ===

INGREDIENTS

3 eggs, at room temperature

1¼ cups (300 ml) warm milk

1 tablespoon (15 ml) olive oil

¾ teaspoon kosher salt

1 cup (120 g) all-purpose flour or bread flour (see Recipe Note)

Nonstick cooking spray

INSTRUCTIONS

In a medium-size bowl, whisk the eggs, milk, oil, and salt until thoroughly combined. Add the flour all at once and whisk until frothy but not overly smooth. The batter should be runny with a few small lumps of flour remaining. Let the batter rest for 30 minutes to 1 hour at room temperature.

Meanwhile, preheat the oven (a conventional oven, not a convection oven) to 400°F (200°C or gas mark 6). Position a rack in the lower-third of the oven to keep the popovers from overbrowning. (Tip: You can also position another rack at the very top of the oven and place a large sheet pan on it to shield the popovers from direct heat.)

Lightly coat a popover pan with cooking spray.

Whisk the batter for a few seconds to get it frothy again, then fill each cup about two-thirds full of batter. Bake for 33 minutes until the popovers are deep golden brown—*do not* open the oven door during this time.

Turn the popovers out of the pan onto a cooling rack. Serve immediately with jam or butter.

RECIPE NOTE

If you're baking at high altitude (elevation over 3,500 feet, or 1 km), the secret to sky-high popovers is using high-protein flour (such as bread flour or high-altitude Hungarian flour) instead of all-purpose flour. Check the nutrition label; it should specify 4 grams of protein to ensure your popovers rise every time.

recipe continues

ACADIA
NATIONAL PARK

AT-HOME TIP

Many popover recipes, including the official recipe from the Jordan Pond House, call for starting with a very hot oven (450°F, 230°C or gas mark 8), then reducing the temperature during baking. This method produces mixed results for me, especially living at four thousand feet (1.2 km) elevation. After much experimentation, I find that using a consistent temperature of 400°F to 410°F (200°C to 210°C or gas mark 6) makes the best popovers every time and also allows me to bake multiple batches one after another.

BOURBON SWEET CORN AND SMOKED TROUT CHOWDER

When Jackson Lake Lodge was completed in 1955, it became the first example of modern architecture inside a national park (a turning point that earned the lodge a National Historic Landmark designation in later years). Though its design was significantly (and controversially) different from all the rustic and romantic "parkitecture" before it, the plan had always been to "bring the outside in."

And sitting in the Mural Room, with its sumptuous views of the Tetons, you can't help but feel like the park comes to *you*. The towering windows certainly elevate the dining experience, but the food speaks for itself. This soup is a standout on the menu, and this recipe is how I reenvisioned their Buffalo Trace bourbon sweet corn and smoked trout chowder. (Feel free to use your favorite bourbon.)

======= MAKES FOUR SERVINGS =======

INGREDIENTS

FOR DILL CRÈME FRAÎCHE

4 ounces (115 g) crème fraîche

1 tablespoon (4 g) minced fresh dill

1½ teaspoons minced fresh chives

1½ teaspoons grated lemon zest

¼ teaspoon kosher salt

Pinch of ground black pepper

FOR CHOWDER

3 tablespoons (42 g) butter

1 yellow onion, diced

2 celery stalks, diced

1 cup (155 g) corn kernels, thawed if frozen

½ cup (120 ml) bourbon

2 cups (480 ml) chicken broth

2 cups (480 ml) clam juice or seafood stock

2 Yukon Gold potatoes, cut into ½-inch (1 cm) chunks

1 teaspoon kosher salt, plus more as needed

½ teaspoon ground black pepper, plus more as needed

1 cup (240 ml) heavy cream

8 ounces (225 g) smoked trout, crumbled

2 tablespoons (8 g) minced fresh dill, plus more for garnishing

INSTRUCTIONS

To make the dill crème fraîche: In a small bowl, whisk all the ingredients until smooth and well blended. Cover and refrigerate until ready to serve.

recipe continues

GRAND TETON
NATIONAL PARK

To make the chowder: In a Dutch oven over medium heat, melt the butter. Add the onion and celery and cook for about 5 minutes, stirring occasionally, until tender. Add the corn and bourbon, increase the heat to medium-high, and bring to a boil. Boil until the liquid has mostly evaporated, then add the broth, clam juice, potatoes, salt, and pepper. Bring the soup to a simmer and cook for about 10 minutes until the potatoes are tender, stirring occasionally and reducing the heat, as needed, to maintain a simmer. Pour in the heavy cream, add the trout and dill, and cook for about 5 minutes until warmed through. Taste and season with more salt and pepper, if desired.

Serve the chowder with a drizzle of dill crème fraîche and a sprinkle of fresh dill on top.

HUCKLEBERRY MARGARITA

It might seem strange at first that Jackson Lake Lodge doesn't actually sit on Jackson Lake. But walk through the building and you'll understand why: The lobby's sixty-foot (18.25 m) windows perfectly frame Jackson Lake and the impossibly craggy Teton Range like a floor-to-ceiling work of art. It's a good day indeed if you end up here, and even better if you're taking in the views from the deck outside the Blue Heron Lounge with a requisite huckleberry margarita in hand.

You might not be able to re-create those views at home, but you can certainly re-create this signature cocktail. My version uses black huckleberries from western Wyoming, but any species of huckleberry will work.

=========== MAKES ONE SERVING ===========

INGREDIENTS

FOR HUCKLEBERRY SYRUP

1 cup (240 ml) water

1 cup (336 g) agave nectar

1 cup (150 g) huckleberries, thawed if frozen

Juice of ½ lemon

FOR MARGARITA

2 lime wedges

Salt

2 ounces (60 ml) silver tequila

1 ounce (30 ml) freshly squeezed lime juice

1 ounce (30 ml) huckleberry syrup

½ ounce (15 ml) Cointreau

Huckleberries for garnishing

INSTRUCTIONS

To make the huckleberry syrup: In a medium-size saucepan over medium-high heat, combine all the ingredients and bring to a boil. Reduce the heat to maintain a simmer and cook for about 10 minutes, stirring occasionally.

Strain the mixture through a fine-mesh sieve, pressing on the fruit with the back of a spoon to get all the liquid out. You should have about 2 cups (480 ml) of syrup. Let cool and transfer to a jar. The syrup will keep, refrigerated, for up to 2 weeks.

To make the margarita: Juice one lime wedge and use the rind to wet the rim of a chilled rocks glass. Pour some salt onto a plate and gently press the wet rim of the glass into the salt.

Fill a cocktail shaker with ice and pour in the tequila, lime juice, huckleberry syrup, and Cointreau. Cover and shake well.

Fill the prepared glass with ice and strain the cocktail into it. Garnish with a spoonful of huckleberries and the remaining lime wedge.

GRAND TETON
NATIONAL PARK

CREEKSIDE CLAM CHOWDER

The quintessential Olympic Peninsula experience starts at Kalaloch Lodge. Inside the weathered gray seaside lodge, Executive Chef John Adams takes the helm at Creekside Restaurant, where—if you're lucky enough to snag a window seat—you can watch waves crashing and shorebirds gathering on the driftwood-strewn beach while enjoying one of the best and freshest clam chowders you've ever had. If you go at the right time of day, you can even dig your own clams from the beach in front of the lodge. With whatever source of clams you have at home, re-create the restaurant's signature chowder in your kitchen with their recipe here.

===== MAKES EIGHT SERVINGS =====

INGREDIENTS

1 pound (454 g) bacon, diced

2 yellow onions, diced

5 celery stalks, diced

6 garlic cloves, minced

5 tablespoons (75 ml) sherry wine

4 cups (960 ml) clam juice

3 Yukon Gold potatoes, diced

4 thyme sprigs

1 bay leaf

1 cup (120 g) all-purpose flour

3½ cups (840 ml) milk

1½ pounds (681 g) raw chopped clams

Salt and ground black pepper

Oyster crackers for serving (optional)

Sourdough bread bowls for serving (optional)

INSTRUCTIONS

In a large saucepan over medium heat, cook the bacon until the bacon fat is mostly liquid. Strain the fat (you should have about 1 cup, or 240 ml) and reserve both the bacon and bacon fat.

Add the onions, celery, garlic, and bacon to the pan and cook for about 5 minutes until the vegetables are tender. Pour in the sherry and cook until the liquid is reduced by half.

Pour in the clam juice and add the potatoes, thyme, and bay leaf and bring the mixture to a boil. Reduce the heat to maintain a simmer and cook for 20 to 25 minutes until the potatoes are tender.

Meanwhile, in a small saucepan over low heat, whisk the reserved bacon fat and flour to blend. Cook for about 5 minutes, whisking, until the mixture thickens to a golden-brown roux. Remove from the heat.

Once the potatoes are tender, add the milk and bring the chowder to a boil. Whisk in the roux, reduce the heat to maintain a simmer, and cook for about 5 minutes. Add the clams, return the chowder to a simmer, and cook for 10 minutes. Season with salt and pepper to taste. Discard the bay leaves and thyme sprigs.

Serve the chowder with oyster crackers on the side (if using). Optionally, ladle the chowder into bread bowls for serving (if using).

OLYMPIC NATIONAL PARK

AT-HOME TIP

If your bacon is on the lean side, melt enough butter with the reserved bacon fat to equal 1 cup (240 ml) total fat before stirring in the flour for the roux.

DUNGENESS CRAB MAC AND BEECHER'S CHEESE

You'll notice a "secret" ingredient in this recipe: sodium citrate. It's an emulsifying salt that turns any type of cheese into the smoothest, most meltable, gooey cheese sauce ever—like movie theater–style nacho cheese. Kalaloch Lodge uses it to elevate the restaurant's mac and cheese game, coating their locally sourced Dungeness crab (caught right off the Olympic Peninsula) in a rich, silky sauce that nearly drips off your fork. You can omit the sodium citrate, but your sauce will have a slightly different consistency.

MAKES SIX TO EIGHT SERVINGS

INGREDIENTS

1 pound (454 g) dried elbow macaroni

4⅓ cups (1 L) milk

3 tablespoons (37 g) sodium citrate

1½ teaspoons chili powder

1½ teaspoons garlic powder

1¼ tablespoons (8.75 g) Old Bay Seasoning, plus more for garnishing

2½ pounds (1.1 kg) Beecher's Flagship cheddar cheese, grated

8 ounces (225 g) Dungeness crabmeat, freshly picked

Minced fresh chives for garnishing

INSTRUCTIONS

In a large saucepan, cook the macaroni according to the package directions. Drain.

In a Dutch oven over medium heat, combine the milk, sodium citrate, chili powder, garlic powder, and Old Bay and stir until the sodium citrate is fully dissolved. Bring to a simmer. Gradually add the cheese and whisk, or use an immersion blender, until smooth. Stir in the cooked macaroni and crabmeat and heat until warmed through.

Garnish with a few pinches of Old Bay and chives before serving.

RECIPE NOTE

You can find sodium citrate online or in restaurant supply stores. A little goes a long way, so buy it once and use it for years.

OLYMPIC NATIONAL PARK

TROUT WITH WILD RICE AND FIGS

Like many other national park lodges, the historic Glacier Park Lodge was built by a railroad company to accommodate tourists arriving on its passenger trains. In keeping with the architectural theme throughout Glacier (deemed the "Switzerland of America"), the Great Northern Railway modeled the lodge after a Swiss chalet. The lobby and dining room officially opened in 1913 and has continuously nourished visitors with hot meals, Montana style. This recipe is courtesy of the Great Northern Dining Room.

=========== MAKES FOUR SERVINGS ===========

INGREDIENTS

FOR THYME BUTTER

4 tablespoons (½ stick, or 56 g) butter

¼ cup (10 g) chopped fresh thyme leaves

FOR WILD RICE

1½ cups (360 ml) chicken broth

½ cup (100 g) raw white rice

¼ cup (40 g) raw wild rice, soaked in water for 3 hours, drained

1 tablespoon (14 g) butter

1 teaspoon kosher salt

½ cup (91 g) diced fresh figs

FOR MAIN COURSE

12 young carrots

½ cup (160 g) maple syrup

Salt and ground black pepper

4 (6-ounce, or 170 g) rainbow trout fillets

4 tablespoons (60 ml) olive oil, divided

INSTRUCTIONS

To make the thyme butter: In a small saucepan over medium heat, melt the butter. Stir in the thyme and simmer for 2 minutes. Remove from the heat and move to a cool place to harden.

To make the wild rice: In a medium-size saucepan, combine the broth, white rice, wild rice, butter, and salt. Bring to a simmer, cover, and cook for about 20 minutes, until the rice is tender and fluffy. Reduce the heat so the rice simmers but doesn't boil over. Stir in the figs, cover, and remove from the heat.

To make the main course: Preheat the oven to 350°F (180°C or gas mark 4).

Place the carrots on a sheet pan. Drizzle the maple syrup over them, sprinkle with a few generous pinches of salt and pepper, and toss to coat. Roast for about 40 minutes, or until the carrots are golden brown and easily pierced with a fork.

Meanwhile, season the trout on both sides with salt and pepper. In a large skillet over medium-high heat, heat 2 tablespoons (30 ml) of oil. Working in two batches, place the trout, flesh-side down, into the skillet to sear. Cook for about 2 minutes, or until the fish releases naturally from the skillet, and flip it. Sear the skin side for 2 minutes. Repeat with the remaining 2 tablespoons (30 ml) of oil and two fillets.

To serve, divide the rice among four plates. Layer three carrots over each mound of rice, followed by a trout fillet. Top with a large spoonful of thyme butter and let it melt over the fish.

GLACIER NATIONAL PARK

AT-HOME TIP

The chef uses young organic carrots in this recipe (about 12 ounces, or 340 g, total). If all you can find are standard carrots, halve them lengthwise so they roast evenly.

BACON-WRAPPED MEAT LOAF

Despite its name, Glacier Park Lodge isn't located inside the park. It stands on the Blackfeet Indian Reservation, marking a point of entry for far-flung chalets and other lodges within the park, and acting as a sort of intermediary between civilization and wilderness. For more than one hundred years, the lodge has attracted legions of visitors coming by train or car to experience the "Crown of the Continent" and has served countless comfort foods and farm-to-table meals inside its rustic log dining room. This recipe is one such meal you might enjoy there, and it comes courtesy of the Great Northern Dining Room.

MAKES SIX SERVINGS

INGREDIENTS

1 tablespoon (15 ml) olive oil

1/2 cup (75 g) diced red bell pepper

1/2 cup (80 g) diced yellow onion

1 1/2 teaspoons minced garlic

2 cups (480 g) ketchup

2 tablespoons (5 g) chopped fresh thyme leaves

2 1/2 pounds (1.1 kg) ground beef

3 eggs, beaten

3/4 cup (37.5 g) panko bread crumbs

1 1/2 teaspoons kosher salt

1 teaspoon ground black pepper

Nonstick cooking spray

1 pound (454 g) bacon slices

INSTRUCTIONS

Preheat the oven to 350°F (180°C or gas mark 4).

Place a large saucepan over medium-high heat and drizzle in the oil. Add the bell pepper, onion, and garlic and cook for about 5 minutes, stirring occasionally, until soft. Stir in the ketchup and thyme and bring to a simmer. Simmer for 10 minutes, then cover and keep warm.

Meanwhile, in a large bowl, combine the ground beef, eggs, panko, salt, and pepper. Add half the ketchup mixture and mix all the ingredients well.

Lightly coat a 9 × 5-inch (23 × 13 cm) loaf pan with cooking spray. Line the pan with bacon and let the ends of the slices hang over the edge of the pan. Press the beef mixture into the pan, then pull the bacon ends over the top to cover the beef. Place the pan on a sheet pan to catch any overspills, cover with aluminum foil, and bake for 40 minutes. Pull the loaf pan out of the oven and drain the fat from one corner of the pan. Place the pan back in the oven and continue baking, uncovered, for 15 minutes, or until the beef is fully cooked and reaches an internal temperature of 160°F (71°C). Drain the fat once more.

Let sit for 5 minutes, then invert the pan over a platter to transfer the meat loaf. Top with the remaining warm ketchup mixture before serving.

GLACIER NATIONAL PARK

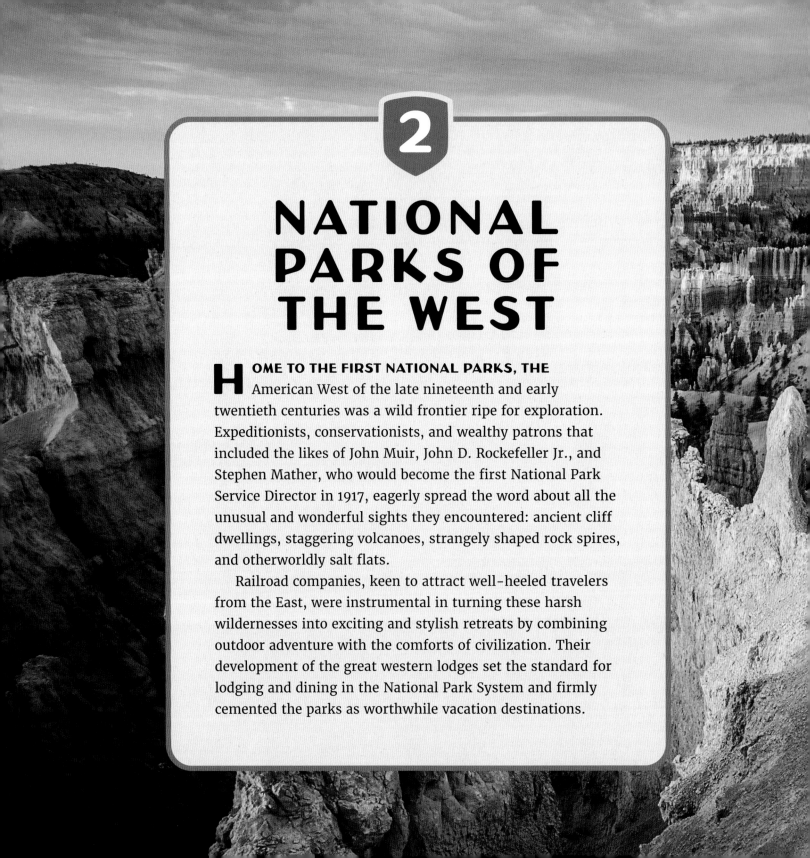

NATIONAL PARKS OF THE WEST

HOME TO THE FIRST NATIONAL PARKS, THE American West of the late nineteenth and early twentieth centuries was a wild frontier ripe for exploration. Expeditionists, conservationists, and wealthy patrons that included the likes of John Muir, John D. Rockefeller Jr., and Stephen Mather, who would become the first National Park Service Director in 1917, eagerly spread the word about all the unusual and wonderful sights they encountered: ancient cliff dwellings, staggering volcanoes, strangely shaped rock spires, and otherworldly salt flats.

Railroad companies, keen to attract well-heeled travelers from the East, were instrumental in turning these harsh wildernesses into exciting and stylish retreats by combining outdoor adventure with the comforts of civilization. Their development of the great western lodges set the standard for lodging and dining in the National Park System and firmly cemented the parks as worthwhile vacation destinations.

Bryce Canyon National Park

Crater Lake National Park

2

SHORTCUT CARAMELIZED ONIONS

Real-deal caramelized onions take up to an hour to make on the stove (see French Onion Soup Gratinée, page 24). But, this simple shortcut turns the onions just soft and sweet enough to trick your taste buds.

- Place a large skillet over medium-high heat and add a drizzle of olive oil, a pat of butter, and one to two onions, thinly sliced lengthwise.

- Cook for 3 to 5 minutes until the onions start to soften, stirring frequently and scraping up the browned bits with a spatula.

- Add a splash of water and continue cooking, stirring, and scraping until the onions are deep brown and reduced to half their volume. Add a little more water, as needed, to keep the onions from burning or drying out. Total time on the stove: 15 to 20 minutes.

PARADISE GRILLED CHEESE SANDWICH

Don't be fooled into thinking this is just another grilled cheese sandwich—it's the *ultimate* grilled cheese sandwich, one so delectable that when I asked Paradise Inn (the one-hundred-plus-year-old historic lodge on Mt. Rainier, designated as one of the "Great Lodges of the West") for their favorite recipe, they didn't hesitate to send me their signature grilled cheese. Stacked with local Washington ingredients, including artisan cheese from Seattle and sweet onions from Walla Walla, it's the perfect balance of savory and sweet.

MAKES ONE SERVING

INGREDIENTS

Butter for spreading

2 slices 9-grain bread

2 ounces (56 g) Dijon apple butter (see Recipe Note)

2 ounces (56 g) shredded Beecher's Flagship cheddar cheese, divided

2 ounces (56 g) thinly sliced Bartlett pear

1 ounce (28 g) thinly sliced Granny Smith apple

1 ounce (28 g) chopped fresh spinach

1 ounce (28 g) caramelized Walla Walla onion (see sidebar)

INSTRUCTIONS

Lightly butter one side of each slice of bread. With the bread butter-side down, spread the apple butter evenly on both slices. Construct the sandwich by sprinkling half the cheese on one slice over the apple butter, then layer the pear, apple, spinach, onion, and remaining cheese on top. Place the second slice of bread over the filling, butter-side up.

Heat a medium-size skillet over medium heat. Add the sandwiches and cook for 2 to 4 minutes until the bread is golden brown and the cheese is starting to melt. Flip the sandwich and cook for 1 to 2 minutes more until the cheese is melted. (It may help to cover the skillet during cooking to completely warm the filling.) Once finished, cut the sandwich in half and serve.

RECIPE NOTE

If you can't find Dijon apple butter, make your own by combining one part Dijon mustard and two parts apple butter.

MT. RAINIER
NATIONAL PARK

BLUEBERRY BASIL FROSÉ

From huckleberries to salmonberries, Mt. Rainier is a forager's paradise. But one of the most abundant wild berries found in the park is the lowbush blueberry, which flanks the trails and carpets the hillsides with ripe, juicy berries in summer. Every sunny slope teems with the delicious fruit, serving as an on-the-go snack for all who roam the park. Fortunately, Mt. Rainier also allows each visitor to bring home a gallon (2.3 kg) of berries each day—an edible souvenir, if you will.

If your berries actually make it home (which is hard to do if you have a pack of hungry hikers with you), try this refreshing rosé. It's a welcome treat after a day of exploring the trails.

MAKES SIX SERVINGS

INGREDIENTS

1 (750 ml) bottle rosé wine

3 cups (360 g) ice

2 cups (310 g) frozen blueberries, plus more for garnishing

¼ cup (50 g) sugar

¼ cup (60 ml) freshly squeezed lemon juice

2 tablespoons (5 g) chopped fresh basil leaves

INSTRUCTIONS

In a blender, combine all the ingredients and blend on high speed until smooth. Divide the frosé among six glasses, garnish with a few blueberries, and serve.

MT. RAINIER
NATIONAL PARK

MARIONBERRY GALETTE

Few people outside of the Pacific Northwest have heard of marionberries. The prized berries, a cross between Chehalem blackberries and olallieberries, are grown exclusively in Oregon and rarely travel outside of the region—a true "born and raised" product of the state, beloved by locals for its sweet-yet-tart flavor. It's hard to go anywhere in Oregon without finding marionberry pies, jams, ice cream, beer, liquor . . . anything you can put a berry in.

Although many parts of the country are known for their regional cuisines, such as West Virginia Soup Beans and Cast-Iron Corn Bread (page 145), Oregon has distinctive ingredients like marionberries, which make even a simple pastry feel like a specialty.

MAKES SIX SERVINGS

INGREDIENTS

All-purpose flour for dusting

1 puff pastry sheet (from a 17.3-ounce, or 490.5 g, package), thawed if frozen

1 egg, lightly beaten with 1 tablespoon (15 ml) water to make an egg wash

1 pound (454 g) marionberries, thawed if frozen

¼ cup (50 g) granulated sugar

¼ cup (42 g) finely chopped crystallized ginger

2 tablespoons (16 g) cornstarch

Juice from ½ lemon

1 tablespoon (14 g) butter, cut into small pieces

Coarse sugar for sprinkling

INSTRUCTIONS

Preheat the oven to 400°F (200°C or gas mark 6). Line a large sheet pan with parchment paper.

Lightly dust a work surface with flour and unroll the puff pastry on it. Using a rolling pin, roll the pastry dough into a 12-inch (30 cm) square. Place the dough on the prepared sheet pan and lightly brush the egg wash all over it.

In a medium-size bowl, stir together the marionberries, granulated sugar, ginger, cornstarch, and lemon juice. Use a slotted spoon to scoop the marionberry mixture out of the bowl, allowing most of the juices to drip off before transferring the berries to the dough. Arrange the berries in the center of the dough, leaving a 2-inch (5 cm) border around the edges. Fold the edges up and over the filling, pressing gently to seal the folds as you work your way around. Scatter the butter over the filling. Brush the egg wash over the edges of the dough, then lightly sprinkle the egg-washed edges with coarse sugar.

Bake for 30 to 35 minutes until the crust is golden brown and puffy. Transfer the galette with the parchment paper to a wire rack and cool completely before slicing and serving.

CRATER LAKE
NATIONAL PARK

MARIONBERRY SMASH

Marionberries are somewhat of an Oregon obsession. When they were introduced in the 1950s by Oregon State University, the berries were widely hailed as the most delicious blackberry cultivar around. Their softness makes it impossible to ship fresh fruit out of state, so the berries are enjoyed locally as soon as they ripen in summer. Oregonians praise the marionberry's perfect balance of sweetness and acidity, which shines through in this sangria-like cocktail.

MAKES ONE SERVING

INGREDIENTS

6 marionberries

2 ounces (60 ml) brandy

2 ounces (60 ml) dry red wine

¾ ounce (22.5 ml) simple syrup

¾ ounce (22.5 ml) freshly squeezed lime juice

INSTRUCTIONS

In a rocks glass, muddle three marionberries. Top with ice and set aside.

Fill a cocktail shaker with ice and pour in the brandy, wine, simple syrup, and lime juice. Cover and shake well. Strain the cocktail into the prepared glass and stir to chill. Garnish with the remaining three marionberries on top.

RECIPE NOTE

Use a 1:1 ratio of sugar to water to make the simple syrup.

CRATER LAKE NATIONAL PARK

GENERAL SHERMAN TURKEY LEGS

Enormous turkey legs aren't solely the stuff of Renaissance fairs and Disney parks. They're also a big, meaty indulgence at Wuksachi Lodge, where they're so grand, they're named after General Sherman—*that* General Sherman, the largest living tree in the world, found just down the road in the Giant Forest of Sequoia.

But don't let their namesake (or the multiday prep) intimidate you. This official recipe from the lodge is mostly hands-off from start to finish. Executive Chef Joe Montgomery coats them in a deliciously sweet glaze made with General Sherman IPA, but you can use your favorite fruity IPA here. You'll also need wood chips or wood chunks for smoking.

══ MAKES EIGHT SERVINGS ══

INGREDIENTS

FOR BRINE

4 quarts (3.8 L) water, divided

2 cups (400 g) granulated sugar

2 cups (450 g) brown sugar

1 cup (240 g) kosher salt

1 whole star anise

1 bay leaf

8 (1- to 1½-pound, or 454 to 681 g) turkey legs

FOR GLAZE

1 (16-ounce, or 480 ml) can General Sherman IPA or any fruity IPA

1 cup (200 g) granulated sugar

⅓ cup (107 g) maple syrup

INSTRUCTIONS

To make the brine: Pour 2 quarts (1.9 L) of water into a large saucepan over high heat and add the remaining brine ingredients. Bring to a boil, stirring occasionally, and cook until the sugars and salt have dissolved. Remove the pot from the heat and let cool. (If you're short on time, add ice to cool the brine faster.)

Place the turkey legs in a large container (one that fits in your refrigerator) and pour the cooled brine over them. Top off with the remaining 2 quarts (1.9 L) of water (you may not use it all, depending on the size of your container), then cover and refrigerate for 24 hours.

Transfer the turkey legs to a wire rack set over a large sheet pan. Refrigerate, uncovered, for 24 hours to air-dry.

Preheat the smoker to 210°F (99°C). Add wood chips or wood chunks of choice, arrange the turkey legs on the grate, and smoke for 6 to 8 hours until the turkey legs reach an internal temperature of 165°F (74°C) in the thickest part of the flesh.

To make the glaze: About 30 minutes before serving, in a medium-size saucepan over medium-high heat, combine all the glaze ingredients. Bring to a rapid boil and boil for 15 to 20 minutes until the liquid is reduced to a thick, sauce-like consistency, stirring occasionally.

Dip each turkey leg in the glaze to evenly coat and serve immediately.

SEQUOIA NATIONAL PARK

AT-HOME TIP

If you don't have a large enough container to fit all the turkey legs, divide them between two large bowls (or a few gallon-size resealable bags) for brining.

AT-HOME TIP

I like using thick, hearty mushrooms for this recipe, because they'll shrink to 30 to 50 percent of their original volume. Feel free to experiment with other types of mushrooms: You can try king oyster, oyster, or shiitake, but keep an eye on them in the oven as baking times vary.

SHROOM JERKY

No other national park is cloaked in mysticism as much as Joshua Tree. The rock band U2 even made a whole album about it. With its namesake trees twisting and stretching toward the sky (like the Biblical figure Joshua reaching his hands up and guiding Mormon settlers to the promised land, as legend has it), the park is said to be chock-full of spiritual vortexes. People flock to this part of the vast Mojave to channel the desert's energy, search for transcendence, shed old versions of themselves, and emerge born again—and incidentally, get lost in a good mind-bending trip.

So, are these magic mushrooms? No—but a taste of this divine jerky alternative might have you re-examining the existence of beef. Shroom jerky has all the chewiness and umami bomb of the real thing. Because mushrooms are like sponges, they soak up flavors really well, giving you plenty of opportunity to play with different levels of acid, salt, spice, and sweetness. Make a batch for your next soul-searching trip to JT (as it's known by the locals).

INGREDIENTS

¼ cup (60 ml) reduced-sodium soy sauce

¼ cup (60 ml) rice wine vinegar

1 tablespoon (15 ml) toasted sesame oil

1 tablespoon (15 g) brown sugar

1 teaspoon sriracha

½ teaspoon smoked paprika

½ teaspoon garlic powder

6 portobello mushrooms, stemmed and cut into ¼-inch (0.6 cm) slices

INSTRUCTIONS

In a small bowl, whisk the soy sauce, vinegar, sesame oil, brown sugar, sriracha, smoked paprika, and garlic powder to blend. Pour the mixture into a gallon (3.8 L)-size resealable zip-top bag and add the mushrooms. Seal the bag and shake to coat thoroughly. Refrigerate to marinate for at least 8 hours, or overnight, turning the bag periodically to redistribute the marinade.

Preheat the oven to 250°F (120°C or gas mark ½) and line a large sheet pan with parchment paper.

One by one, remove the mushrooms from the bag, letting excess marinade drip into the bag, and place on the prepared sheet pan, arranging them in a single layer without overlapping. Bake for 1 hour. Flip the mushrooms and bake for 30 to 90 minutes more until the pieces are dried and shrunken to nearly half their original size. The mushrooms should have a chewy texture with crisp edges. If you prefer a softer texture, bake them for less time; if you like your jerky firmer, leave them in the oven a bit longer.

Let cool completely before serving. Refrigerate any leftovers in an airtight container for up to 2 weeks.

JOSHUA TREE
NATIONAL PARK

DATE NUT BREAD

Date nut bread is one of those things that everyone who comes to Death Valley has to have. Its history in the park runs deep: The house-baked bread has been served at The Oasis at Death Valley and sold in the general store since the 1930s. Up until the mid-1990s, dates grown locally at Furnace Creek were used for the resort's bread.

Over time, several recipes have been published for Death Valley's legendary date nut bread, but I'm sharing my version here, which makes a moist, dense bread packed with sweet dates and crunchy walnuts, perfect with a smear of cream cheese and a mug of hot tea.

MAKES 1 (9 × 5-INCH, OR 23 × 13 CM) LOAF

INGREDIENTS

4 tablespoons (½ stick, or 56 g) butter, at room temperature, plus more for greasing

2 cups (356 g) chopped pitted dates

1 cup (240 ml) very hot water

½ cup (112.5 g) packed brown sugar

¾ teaspoon kosher salt

½ teaspoon baking soda

1 egg

1 tablespoon (15 ml) bourbon or brandy

1 teaspoon vanilla extract

1¾ cups (210 g) all-purpose flour

1½ teaspoons baking powder

½ teaspoon ground cinnamon (optional)

1 cup (120 g) chopped toasted walnuts

INSTRUCTIONS

Preheat the oven to 350°F (180°C or gas mark 4). Lightly coat a 9 × 5-inch (23 × 13 cm) loaf pan with butter and line it with parchment paper.

In a medium-size bowl, stir together the dates, hot water, brown sugar, butter, salt, and baking soda. Let sit for 15 minutes to soften the dates.

Whisk in the egg, bourbon, and vanilla. Add the flour, baking powder, and cinnamon (if using) and stir until the mixture is smooth and well blended. Fold in the walnuts.

Pour the batter into the prepared pan, smooth the top, and bake for 55 to 65 minutes, loosely covering the pan with aluminum foil about 35 minutes into baking to prevent overbrowning. The bread is done when a toothpick inserted in the center comes out clean (a few moist crumbs are fine).

Let cool for 15 minutes, then gently turn the bread out of the pan to finish cooling completely before serving.

DEATH VALLEY NATIONAL PARK

AT-HOME TIP

Bourbon (or brandy) is used as a flavor enhancer in this recipe; it's fine to omit it, or substitute a different type of liquor, such as rum, Grand Marnier, or Cognac—experiment to see how each one gives a slightly different nuance to the flavor.

DATE SHAKE

Fun fact: The site of what is now The Ranch at Death Valley used to be a farming operation named Greenland Ranch. In the early 1920s, the ranch received free date palm trees from a defunct U.S. Department of Agriculture project in Arizona, which decided to test Death Valley for date farming. The ranch was able to produce two hundred tons (181 metric tons) of the sticky-sweet fruit annually from 1,500 date palm trees, and dates began popping up on every restaurant menu at the resort. For decades, date shakes have been served at The Oasis at Death Valley as a cooling respite from the desert's soaring temperatures. This is my take on the popular treat!

─────── **MAKES TWO SERVINGS** ───────

INGREDIENTS

1 cup (178 g) chopped pitted dates (see Recipe Note)

¾ cup (180 ml) very hot water

2 to 3 large scoops vanilla ice cream

INSTRUCTIONS

In a small bowl, soak the dates in the hot water for 10 to 15 minutes until softened. Transfer the bowl to the freezer for a few minutes to cool completely.

Pour the dates and their soaking liquid into a blender and blend on high speed until a thick puree forms. Add the ice cream and blend on low speed until smooth. Pour into two chilled tall glasses to serve.

RECIPE NOTE

You can use Medjool or Deglet Noor dates for this recipe. I prefer Medjool because they have a sweeter, more intense date flavor. Be sure to use a creamy, high-quality ice cream for the best shake; my personal favorite is vanilla bean.

DEATH VALLEY
NATIONAL PARK

BLUE CHEESE-STUFFED DATES WITH PROSCIUTTO

Though not native to California, pomegranates (dubbed the "fruits of the desert") thrive in arid conditions with lots of sun. So, it's not surprising that, historically, they were cultivated in the Death Valley region in scattered spots throughout the Panamint Valley, including the infamous Barker Ranch. The hardy, jewel-toned fruit is also grown in the gardens at The Oasis at Death Valley, where it's one of the chefs' prominent local ingredients.

My favorite on the menu? Their signature stuffed dates drizzled with a pomegranate reduction—the sweet and savory combo is out of this world. This recipe is adapted from the one served at The Inn Dining Room.

MAKES SIX SERVINGS

INGREDIENTS

FOR POMEGRANATE REDUCTION

2 cups (480 ml) bottled pomegranate juice

1 teaspoon sugar

1 teaspoon kosher salt

FOR STUFFED DATES

24 large dates

6 ounces (170 g) sharp blue cheese

5 ounces (140 g) thinly sliced prosciutto

Microgreens for garnishing

Pomegranate seeds for garnishing

INSTRUCTIONS

Preheat the oven to 400°F (200°C or gas mark 6).

To make the pomegranate reduction: In a small saucepan over medium-high heat, combine the pomegranate juice, sugar, and salt and bring to a boil. Boil for about 30 minutes until the liquid is reduced to ⅓ cup (80 ml). Keep warm until ready to use.

To make the stuffed dates: With a paring knife, cut a small slit lengthwise in each date and remove the pit. Fill each date's cavity with a small piece of blue cheese and press the date over the cheese to close.

Cut twenty-four strips of prosciutto as wide as the dates are long and wrap a strip around each date twice. Pierce the dates with toothpicks to hold the prosciutto in place. Arrange the dates on a sheet pan and bake for about 8 minutes until the prosciutto is browned and the cheese starts to melt.

Garnish each serving of dates with a small handful of microgreens, a sprinkle of pomegranate seeds, and a light drizzle of the pomegranate reduction.

DEATH VALLEY NATIONAL PARK

BUTTERSCOTCH MARTINI WITH BOOZY WHIPPED CREAM

Ponderosa pines are almost everywhere you turn in Bryce Canyon, and they're hard to miss. As one of the tallest trees in the Southwest, ponderosas rise from the canyon floor and poke their way out above the hoodoos, capable of soaring to incredible heights of 150 feet (46 m) or more. They're also easily identified by their smell: Press your nose against the bark and you get an undeniably delicious whiff of butterscotch—some even say vanilla or fresh-baked cookies.

The towering trees are the inspiration for this butterscotch martini, a strong after-dinner drink that's dessert in itself.

=== **MAKES ONE SERVING** ===

INGREDIENTS

FOR WHIPPED CREAM

1 cup (240 ml) cold heavy cream

3 tablespoons (21 g) powdered sugar

1 to 2 ounces (30 to 60 ml) Irish cream liqueur

FOR MARTINI

2 ounces (60 ml) butterscotch schnapps

2 ounces (60 ml) vanilla vodka

2 ounces (60 ml) Irish cream liqueur

INSTRUCTIONS

To make the whipped cream: Place a medium-size bowl or the bowl of your stand mixer and the beaters in the refrigerator to chill for about 30 minutes.

In the cold bowl, combine the cold heavy cream and powdered sugar. Using a handheld mixer, or stand mixer fitted with the whisk attachment, whisk on medium-low speed for 5 to 7 minutes until stiff peaks form. Slowly whisk in the Irish cream, $\frac{1}{2}$ ounce (15 ml) at a time, tasting after each addition until the flavor is to your liking.

To make the martini: Fill a cocktail shaker with ice and pour in the schnapps, vodka, and Irish cream liqueur. Cover and shake well, then strain the martini into a chilled martini glass. Top with the prepared whipped cream. (For the perfect swirl, use a piping bag, or fill a resealable zip-top bag with whipped cream and snip off a bottom corner to create a makeshift piping bag.)

Refrigerate any unused whipped cream, covered, for up to 2 days.

BRYCE CANYON NATIONAL PARK

MIXED BERRY MINI PIES

A visit to Capitol Reef isn't complete without a pit stop at the Gifford Homestead, a restored farmhouse originally built in 1908 and occupied until 1969. Today, the landmark has been converted into a gift shop selling handmade home goods reminiscent of the pioneer era, including jams and jellies, quilts, wooden spoons, and, perhaps most popular of all, individual-size fruit pies. The store sells tens of thousands of pies every year, baked locally in the town of Torrey, and this recipe is my homemade version of those famous treats.

==== MAKES SIX (5-INCH, OR 13 CM) PIES ====

INGREDIENTS

FOR CRUSTS

All-purpose flour for dusting

4 refrigerated premade piecrusts

1 tablespoon (15 ml) milk

Coarse sugar for sprinkling

FOR PIE FILLING

¾ cup (150 g) granulated sugar

¼ cup (32 g) cornstarch

½ teaspoon ground cinnamon

2 cups (250 g) fresh raspberries

2 cups (290 g) fresh blueberries

2 cups (290 g) fresh blackberries

1 tablespoon (15 ml) freshly squeezed lemon juice

1 teaspoon vanilla extract

INSTRUCTIONS

Preheat the oven to 400°F (200°C or gas mark 6). Lightly dust a baking sheet with flour.

To make the crusts: Lightly dust a work surface with flour and unroll one piecrust on it. Using a rolling pin, roll the crust into a ⅛-inch (0.3 cm)-thick circle, then use a 6-inch (15 cm) cookie cutter to cut out two rounds. Gather and reroll the scraps into another ⅛-inch (0.3 cm)-thick circle, then cut one additional 6-inch (15 cm) round. Repeat with the remaining three crusts, for a total of twelve rounds.

Place six rounds on the prepared baking sheet, separating the layers with plastic wrap as needed, cover with more plastic wrap, and refrigerate until needed for the top crusts.

Fit the remaining six rounds in the bottoms and up the sides of six (5-inch, or 13 cm) aluminum foil tart pans, pressing firmly. With a fork, prick the bottoms and sides several times. Place the tart pans on a baking sheet.

Bake the tart shells for 6 to 8 minutes until they are just dry and only partially baked. Remove from the oven.

To make the pie filling: In a large bowl, combine the granulated sugar, cornstarch, and cinnamon. Stir in the raspberries, blueberries, blackberries, lemon juice, and vanilla until well coated. Use a slotted spoon to scoop the fruit mixture out of the bowl, allowing most of the juices to drip into the bowl before evenly dividing the fruit among the par-baked crusts.

Remove the top crusts from the refrigerator. Cover each tart pan with a crust and crimp the edges with your fingers so they stop just before the edges of the tin. Using a knife, make a few small slits in the top crust so steam can vent. Brush the tops with milk and sprinkle lightly with coarse sugar.

recipe continues

CAPITOL REEF
NATIONAL PARK

Return the pies to the baking sheet and bake for about 40 minutes until the crusts are golden brown and the filling is bubbly. Cover the pies with a large sheet of foil halfway through baking to prevent the crusts from getting too brown.

Cool the pies for at least 2 hours before serving.

AT-HOME TIP

If you don't have a 6-inch (15 cm) cookie cutter, use the rim of a similar-size bowl instead. Any type of coarse sugar will work for sprinkling on top, including Sugar In The Raw turbinado sugar, sparkling sugar, and decorative sugar for baking.

6 BENTO BOX IDEAS FOR YOUR NATIONAL PARK HIKE

Let's be honest, national park concessioners don't always have the most appetizing options when you need to fuel up for a hike (not to mention the hassle of finding a concessioner near the trailhead or dealing with long lines in summer). That's why I like to pack my own "brown bag" before heading out for the day: I can choose healthy snacks (especially ones I know my kids will eat) and create a tasty, energy-packed portable meal around our family's needs and cravings. But instead of a brown bag, I do a bento box.

Bento boxes are perfect for hiking because they're easy to carry and compartmentalize your food without excess packaging—no more smushed sandwiches or soggy crackers. They're also made for people who hate having their food commingle! Modern-day bento boxes come in all shapes and sizes; some have utensils incorporated into the design, and some are collapsible once you're done eating. I prefer stainless-steel versions because they don't hold odors or stains, but plastic bento boxes are a better choice if you want to reduce your pack weight on the trail.

So, instead of reaching for an uninspiring energy bar next time, pack a bento box. Here are six ideas to take along on your journey. (And remember: Always pack a little more food than you think you'll need, as sometimes you end up hungrier or stay on the trail longer than you intended.)

HUNGRY HIKER BENTO BOX

This bento box is perfect for a longer hike where you can stop for lunch and enjoy the view. Start with your favorite sandwich or wrap, a chicken or tuna salad that you can scoop with crackers, or a zesty pasta salad or quinoa salad. Pack your choice of fresh fruits and vegetables: I like apple slices, berries, clementines, cherry tomatoes, cucumber slices, and mini bell peppers. Then, add something salty and crunchy, like pretzels, nuts, or cheese puffs. If you have room for dessert, throw in a bite-size brownie, some fudge, or a gourmet marshmallow.

CHARCUTERIE BENTO BOX

Going on a date hike? All you need are a couple cans of wine (hey, don't judge—they've come a long way) and this bento spread. Assemble your favorite crackers, cured meats (I like to pack a mild option like prosciutto as well as a spicy option like capicola), Boursin cheese or sliced cheese, olives, pickles, grapes, and strawberries. If you're feeling fancy, add a good stoneground mustard and don't forget your Swiss army knife to spread it with. It doesn't get any more romantic than that!

CRUDITÉS BENTO BOX

You know those veggie-and-dip platters you always see at parties? This is the same idea, but you can pack things you'll actually eat (and not the cardboard-like cauliflower that's been sitting out too long). Choose one or two dips: French onion dip, hummus, Pimento Cheese (page 152), smoked salmon dip, or spinach and artichoke dip. Then, pack a variety of veggies to dip: baby cucumbers, carrot sticks, mini bell peppers, radishes, or snap peas. I sometimes like to include other snacks for added texture and sustenance, like dried cranberries, parmesan crisps, pistachios, pretzel sticks, or raisins.

MEZZE BENTO BOX

Mezze is an assortment of Mediterranean finger foods. You'll notice that a lot of these ingredients can work with my other bento box ideas, and there's no reason you can't mix and match. Think beyond the usual olives, pita, and hummus and consider packing baba ghanoush, tahini, or tzatziki; dolmas, roasted red peppers, or stuffed peppadews; marinated artichoke hearts, marinated feta, or roasted garlic; cucumbers, radishes, or tomatoes; and pita chips, flatbread crackers, or crispy chickpeas. The beauty of mezze is that it's meant for sharing, so put together a few bento boxes to graze on family style.

LOX BENTO BOX

This bento is like a bagel and lox, but without the bagel. It's ideal for a morning outing or midday snack and is a quality source of protein. Start with a good smoked salmon, then grab a stack of crackers ("everything"-seasoned crackers are perfect for this), a flavorful cream cheese (like onion, garlic, or chives), and tomato slices. Sometimes, I even throw in a few sliced red onions or capers—you can keep all these ingredients tidy with bento cups or silicone baking cups that fit inside your bento box.

PROTEIN BOOST BENTO BOX

This bento is inspired by the snack trays you get on airplanes. But, you can make yours better! Pack a hard-boiled egg or two, a handful of cheese cubes, salami, peanuts, almonds (try something fun like tamari almonds or wasabi almonds), grapes, apple slices, and a packet of your favorite peanut butter or nut or seed butter (or Nutella, if you're feeling decadent). The protein-rich assortment gives you good starter fuel for those sunrise missions or a much-needed boost when you've still got miles to go.

STONE FRUIT CLAFOUTIS

Although Capitol Reef is famed for its geologic formations and fossils, visitors venturing off the trail will find something unique: remnants of the pioneer community of Fruita, where orchards planted by Mormon settlers in the late 1800s still thrive. Some orchards contain heirloom varieties of fruit found nowhere else in the world! The National Park Service maintains these orchards and offers U-pick fruits in summer and fall, with proceeds going to their continuing preservation.

This simple treat is a tribute to the fresh, tree-ripened stone fruits of Capitol Reef. The warm, golden custard is one of the easiest and most forgiving recipes you can make, and it's versatile enough to enjoy for breakfast, lunch, or dessert.

MAKES SIX TO EIGHT SERVINGS

INGREDIENTS

2 tablespoons (28 g) butter

3 eggs

1 cup (240 ml) milk

6 tablespoons (75 g) granulated sugar

1 teaspoon vanilla extract

1 teaspoon grated lemon zest

½ teaspoon kosher salt

½ cup (60 g) all-purpose flour

2 cups (340 g; weight varies) halved, pitted, and sliced stone fruit (such as peaches, cherries, or apricots)

2 teaspoons brandy

Powdered sugar for dusting (optional)

Vanilla ice cream for serving (optional)

INSTRUCTIONS

Preheat the oven to 350°F (180°C or gas mark 4).

In a 10-inch (25 cm) ovenproof skillet over medium heat, melt the butter, swirling it around to evenly coat the skillet. Turn off the heat.

In a blender, combine the eggs, milk, granulated sugar, vanilla, lemon zest, and salt. Blend for about 2 minutes until frothy. Add the flour and blend just until combined. Pour the batter into the hot skillet.

Scatter the fruit in a single layer in the skillet and drizzle with the brandy.

Bake for 30 to 40 minutes until the top is puffed and lightly golden brown. Let cool slightly, then dust with powdered sugar (if using).

For dessert, add a scoop of ice cream (if using) to each serving.

CAPITOL REEF
NATIONAL PARK

NAVAJO FRY BREAD

You can't walk very far in Mesa Verde, or anywhere in the Four Corners, without coming across a Navajo staple: fry bread. Though it's often associated with "traditional" Native American cuisine, the puffy, crunchy, chewy bread wasn't a part of their diet until the mid-1800s when Native American tribes were forced onto reservations. Unable to hunt game or grow vegetable crops, they created fry bread with their government rations of flour, lard, and sugar.

Despite its troubling origins, fry bread has become a symbol of the People's survival and perseverance and is now a favorite indulgence all over the Southwest. You can make Navajo Tacos (page 39) with fry bread, dip the bread in soups or stews, or dust with powdered sugar or cinnamon for a sweet snack.

MAKES SIX FRY BREADS

INGREDIENTS

½ cup (120 ml) milk

½ cup (120 ml) water

2 cups (240 g) all-purpose flour, plus more for kneading

2 teaspoons baking powder

½ teaspoon kosher salt

Vegetable oil for frying

INSTRUCTIONS

In a small saucepan over medium-low heat, combine the milk and water and heat until warm.

In a medium-size bowl, combine the flour, baking powder, and salt. Stir in the warm milk mixture to make a dough. Lightly dust a work surface with flour and place the dough on it. Knead the dough until it is soft, smooth, and no longer sticky. Do not overknead. Add more flour, as needed, if the dough is too wet. Transfer the dough back to the bowl and let it rest for 15 minutes.

Meanwhile, pour the oil into a large deep skillet to a depth of 1 inch (2.5 cm). Heat the oil until a deep-fat thermometer registers 360°F (182°C), or the end of a wooden spoon sizzles when dipped into the hot oil.

Divide the dough into six equal portions and roll each portion into a ball. Flatten each ball with the palm of your hand into a thin disk, about 6 inches (15 cm) in diameter.

Working in batches, fry the disks in the hot oil for 1 to 2 minutes per side until they puff up and turn golden brown. Transfer to paper towels to drain. Serve the fry bread hot or warm.

DID YOU KNOW

The popularity of Navajo fry bread is so far-reaching that other tribes have adopted and put their own spin on it. Indian fry bread—or simply, fry bread—can be found beyond the Navajo Nation and was named the official state bread of South Dakota in 2005.

MESA VERDE
NATIONAL PARK

SAGUARO FRUIT SALSA

When you think of a cactus, you probably picture a giant saguaro: a thick spiny column with two arms that stretch out like a candelabra. This colossal cactus is a universal symbol of the American Southwest and can be found all over southern Arizona and Saguaro National Park, which preserves a portion of unspoiled Sonoran Desert and the iconic cacti. (At last count, it's estimated that there are just under two million saguaros in the park.)

In summer, the saguaro's fragrant white flowers give way to sweet red fruits that taste faintly of strawberries. If you don't have a saguaro growing in your yard, you can find the cactus fruits at farmer's markets and specialty grocers throughout the region. Try them in this boldly flavored, summer-ripened fruit salsa, which adds just the right amount of zing to fish, chicken, or chips and dip.

=== MAKES 2 CUPS (500 G) ===

INGREDIENTS

½ cup (120 ml) white wine vinegar

¼ cup (80 g) honey

¼ teaspoon red pepper flakes

¼ cup (29 g) thinly sliced red onion

¾ cup (112.5 g) diced watermelon

½ cup (90 g) coarsely chopped saguaro fruit (see Preparation Tip)

½ cup (87.5 g) diced mango

INSTRUCTIONS

In a small bowl, stir together the vinegar, honey, and red pepper flakes until well blended. Add the onion and let soak for at least 10 minutes.

In another small bowl, combine the watermelon, saguaro, and mango. Drizzle the vinegar-onion mixture over the fruit and toss gently to coat.

PREPARATION TIP

If the saguaro fruit is not already split, halve it lengthwise, then scoop out the flesh with a spoon and discard the skin.

SAGUARO
NATIONAL PARK

CACTUS CRISPS WITH CILANTRO-LIME CREMA

Nearly every plant species surrounding Carlsbad Caverns has spines or thorns on it, and prickly pear cacti are among the most familiar. The low-growing clumps of green paddles line the entrance road to the park, providing food and habitat for all manner of wildlife that roam above the labyrinth of spectacular cave rooms. The cactus's intimidating spikes mask an otherwise tender and juicy (or should I say, mucilaginous?) flesh, with a flavor that some might describe as a little sour, a little bitter, or mildly earthy like asparagus. If you can't find fresh cactus paddles, you can use jarred "nopalitos" in a pinch.

MAKES FOUR SERVINGS

INGREDIENTS

FOR CREMA

1 cup (240 g) Mexican crema

¼ cup (4 g) packed fresh cilantro

2 tablespoons (28 g) mayonnaise

Grated zest of 1 lime

Juice of 1 lime

½ teaspoon kosher salt

1 garlic clove, peeled

1 teaspoon garlic powder

1 teaspoon paprika

FOR CACTUS CRISPS

Vegetable oil for frying

1 cup (120 g) all-purpose flour

1 teaspoon kosher salt

1 teaspoon ground black pepper

1 teaspoon ground cumin

1 teaspoon cayenne pepper

4 or 5 cactus paddles, thorns removed and edges trimmed (see Charred Cactus and Corn Salad, Preparation Tip, page 116)

INSTRUCTIONS

To make the crema: In a food processor, combine all the crema ingredients and pulse until smooth and well blended, stopping to scrape down the sides of the bowl with a rubber spatula as necessary. Transfer the crema to a small bowl and set aside.

To make the cactus crisps: Pour the oil into a large deep skillet to a depth of 1 inch (2.5 cm). Heat the oil until a deep-fat thermometer registers 360°F (182°C), or the end of a wooden spoon sizzles when dipped into the hot oil.

In a large shallow bowl, whisk the flour and all the seasonings to blend. Slice each cactus paddle into 3 × ¾-inch (7.5 × 2 cm) strips and dip each into the flour mixture until coated on all sides.

Working in batches, fry the cactus strips in the hot oil for 2 to 3 minutes until golden brown and crispy. Transfer to paper towels to drain.

Serve warm with the cilantro-lime crema on the side for dipping.

CARLSBAD CAVERNS NATIONAL PARK

CHARRED CACTUS AND CORN SALAD

Prickly pear cacti grow abundantly in the northern Chihuahuan Desert, where the massive underground chambers of Carlsbad Caverns were first discovered. The prickly pear cactus is also one of the most recognizable for its edible paddles, which have a unique flavor that toes the line between tart and bitter and an oozing texture reminiscent of okra. Harvested wild or homegrown, cactus paddles are best in spring, when they're at their juiciest, but store-bought cactus (also called nopal) will have most of the hard prickly work done for you.

MAKES SIX SERVINGS

INGREDIENTS

4 cactus paddles, thorns removed and edges trimmed (see Preparation Tip)

4 ears corn, husked

Olive oil for brushing

Salt and ground black pepper

Juice of 1 lime

1/3 cup (50 g) crumbled Cotija cheese

1/4 cup (4 g) chopped fresh cilantro

INSTRUCTIONS

Preheat the grill to medium-high heat (about 400°F, or 200°C).

Slice each cactus paddle lengthwise into 1/2-inch (1 cm) strips, stopping 1 inch (2.5 cm) before you reach the end. The paddle should resemble a fan.

Lightly coat the cactus and corn on all sides with oil and season with salt and pepper. Arrange them on the grill directly over the heat. Grill the cactus for about 5 minutes per side until tender and evenly charred. Grill the corn for about 10 minutes total, rotating the cobs every 3 minutes until the kernels are soft and lightly charred.

Transfer the cactus paddles and corn to a cutting board and let them cool enough to handle. Cut each cactus strip into bite-size pieces and slice the kernels off the cobs.

In a large bowl, gently stir together the chopped cactus, corn kernels, lime juice, Cotija, and cilantro. Season with salt and pepper to taste.

PREPARATION TIP

Store-bought cactus paddles usually have the large thorns removed, but you'll need to remove the remaining prickly nubs before cooking. You can rub them off under running water with a scrubby kitchen sponge, or use a knife to slice off the nubs. Then, cut a thin slice off the edge, all the way around, to remove the rest of the nubs.

CARLSBAD CAVERNS
NATIONAL PARK

3

NATIONAL PARKS OF THE MIDWEST AND EAST

COMPARED TO THE WESTERN UNITED STATES, the Midwest and the East have far fewer national parks, though it's certainly not for lack of scenery. Aquatic wonderlands, river valleys, and rolling hills (not to mention unparalleled fall color) are characteristic of national parks east of the Rockies. So, why the disparity? It simply came down to development—or lack thereof.

Whereas the Wild West was uninhabited by white settlers, inaccessible, cheap, and widely available in the 1800s, eastern regions were largely populated and privately owned, making it trickier (and more expensive) for the government to acquire vast tracts of land. Through legal and political maneuvering (not to mention local agitation), national parks became established slowly in the East, but today, some of the region's most picturesque landscapes remain in ordinary people's backyards.

Cuyahoga Valley National Park

Badlands National Park

3

APFELKUCHEN

If you've never been to North Dakota, you might be surprised to learn that one of the state's beloved comfort foods is a German dessert that's like a mash-up of cake, pie, and custard. German immigrants from Russia brought kuchen to the Dakota Territory in the late 1800s, and these recipes have been passed down through generations of families—some as closely guarded secrets!

You'll find endless variations of sweet and savory kuchens in bakeries and restaurants all over the region, including Cedar Pass Lodge at Badlands. My version of apfelkuchen, which translates to "apple cake," is simple enough for even a nonbaker to try and serves as a good jumping-off point for your own kuchen experimentation.

===== MAKES EIGHT SERVINGS =====

INGREDIENTS

1¾ (210 g) cups all-purpose flour

½ cup (100 g) granulated sugar, divided

8 tablespoons (1 stick, or 112 g) cold butter, cut into small pieces

½ teaspoon kosher salt

¼ teaspoon baking powder

3 cups (330 g) thinly sliced apples

1 teaspoon ground cinnamon

2 egg yolks

1 cup (240 g) sour cream

Powdered sugar for dusting (optional)

INSTRUCTIONS

Preheat the oven to 400°F (200°C or gas mark 6).

In a food processor, combine the flour, ¼ cup (50 g) of sugar, the butter, salt, and baking powder and pulse until the mixture resembles fine crumbs. Scoop the dough into a 9-inch (23 cm) pie pan. Using your hands, press the dough evenly across the bottom and up the sides of the pan to form a crust.

Arrange the apple slices on the crust in an overlapping pinwheel pattern. Sprinkle the remaining ¼ cup (50 g) of sugar and the cinnamon over the apples. Bake for 15 minutes.

Meanwhile, in a small bowl, whisk the egg yolks and sour cream until well blended. Pour the mixture evenly over the apples and bake for about 25 minutes until the custard is set and starting to brown slightly.

Before serving, dust with powdered sugar (if using). The apfelkuchen can be served hot, cold, or at room temperature.

BADLANDS
NATIONAL PARK

MINNESOTA WILD RICE SOUP

Wild rice was first discovered on Lake Superior by the Ojibwe People in the 1600s. The aquatic grass, whose edible grain is still harvested by hand, in a canoe, in northern Minnesota, is such an important part of the state's history that it was designated as Minnesota's official grain. It's also the star ingredient in wild rice soup, the state's unofficial-yet-should-be-official dish—especially since it's basically a hotdish, and nothing's more Minnesotan than that.

According to the *Star Tribune*, the original wild rice soup was created in the mid-1970s at the old Orion Room restaurant in downtown Minneapolis. Since then, it's become a staple in many parts of the Great Lakes region, and you'll usually find wild rice soup on the menu at Kettle Falls Hotel in Voyageurs National Park. This is my take on the classic soup, which is delicious on its own but even better with a side of crusty bread.

INGREDIENTS

1 cup (160 g) raw wild rice

4 tablespoons (½ stick, or 56 g) butter

1 yellow onion, diced

3 carrots, diced

3 celery stalks, diced

1½ cups (345 g) sliced cremini mushrooms

3 teaspoons (15 g) kosher salt, divided, plus more as needed

3 tablespoons (22.5 g) all-purpose flour

1 cup (240 ml) dry white wine

6 cups (1.4 L) chicken broth

4 thyme sprigs

2 bay leaves

2 cups (280 g) shredded rotisserie chicken

½ cup (120 ml) heavy cream

1 teaspoon ground black pepper, plus more as needed

Chopped fresh parsley for garnishing

¼ cup (27.5 g) slivered almonds, toasted

INSTRUCTIONS

Different types of wild rice (wild-harvested vs. cultivated) have vastly different cooking times, so cook the rice according to the package directions. Once cooked, the grains generally triple in volume, so you should have about 3 cups (495 g) of cooked wild rice.

recipe continues

VOYAGEURS
NATIONAL PARK

Meanwhile, in a Dutch oven over medium heat, melt the butter. Add the onion and cook for 3 to 5 minutes until soft and translucent. Add the carrots, celery, and mushrooms and sprinkle with 1 teaspoon salt. Cook for about 15 minutes until the vegetables are tender, the mushrooms have browned, and the liquid has mostly evaporated, stirring occasionally. (Be patient! Cooking the vegetables this long will help develop the most flavor in your soup.) Sprinkle the flour over the vegetables and stir until no dry flour remains.

Increase the heat to medium-high and pour in the wine. Simmer until the liquid has reduced by about half, stirring and scraping the browned bits from the bottom of the pot.

Add the broth, thyme, and bay leaves. Bring to a boil, then reduce the heat to maintain a simmer and cook for 20 minutes. Stir in the cooked wild rice, chicken, heavy cream, remaining 2 teaspoons of salt, and pepper. Cook for about 5 minutes until warmed through.

Discard the thyme and bay leaves. Taste the soup and season with more salt or pepper, if desired. Garnish each bowl with a sprinkle of parsley and almonds before serving.

DID YOU KNOW

Most stores carry blackened wild rice (also called cultivated, farmed, or paddy rice), but if you search online or head to a specialty market, you'll encounter another type: naturally grown, hand-harvested wild rice (also called lake rice, river rice, or manoomin) with unevenly colored grains in shades of gold to brown. Although they come from the same plant, the difference in color is a result of how they're processed after harvesting.

The good stuff—hand-harvested wild rice—is visibly different, cooks in half the time, costs double the price, and has a more delicate texture and toasty flavor.

WILD THIMBLEBERRY JAM

Isle Royale may be the country's least visited national park in the lower forty-eight, but that doesn't mean it lacks in beauty. The park is a remote wilderness island in the surging waters of Lake Superior, and access is only by seaplane or boat. People who are up for the adventure get rewarded in late summer to fall with an abundance of ripe thimbleberries on the trails.

The cap-shaped berries resemble raspberries but are more intensely sweet-tart in flavor; think raspberry-flavored candy. They're so delicate that they can't really be sold fresh, but if you're able to harvest a few cups in the wild, enjoy them immediately—then, turn the rest of that goodness into jam. It's a popular (and expensive) souvenir from the Upper Peninsula of Michigan, and very worth making at home yourself.

———— MAKES 1 HALF-PINT (320 G) JAR ————

INGREDIENTS

2 cups (290 g) thimbleberries

1 cup (200 g) sugar

Pictured: Little toasts topped with mascarpone, thimbleberry jam, and a sprinkling of fresh thyme.

INSTRUCTIONS

In a medium-size saucepan over medium-high heat, stir together the thimbleberries and sugar. Bring the mixture to a full rolling boil, stirring constantly to keep the berries from sticking and burning. Boil for 2 to 3 minutes until thickened.

Remove from the heat and let cool, then ladle the jam into a clean jar and refrigerate for up to 3 months.

AT-HOME TIP

Thimbleberries are fragile and can turn to mush if washed like other berries. To clean them, spread the thimbleberries across a surface and handpick any insects or debris out of the "caps." If needed, carefully gather them into a colander and *very gently* rinse them. Let drip-dry in the sink before using.

ISLE ROYALE
NATIONAL PARK

SUPERIOR WHITEFISH TACOS

Isle Royale is an angler's paradise, home to more than forty species of fish. But lake whitefish (a member of the trout family) is one of the most plentiful in the cold, deep waters of Lake Superior. Anglers in the park are often rewarded with the flaky, mild-flavored fish, a perfect choice for people who aren't keen on things that taste "fishy." It easily adapts to almost any recipe—like these Baja-style fish tacos, where the smoky, spicy sauce pulls everything together.

===== MAKES FOUR TO SIX SERVINGS =====

INGREDIENTS

Vegetable oil for frying

FOR BAJA SAUCE

½ cup (120 g) Mexican crema

2 tablespoons (30 g) adobo sauce

Grated zest of ½ lime

Juice of ½ lime

FOR BEER BATTER

1 cup (120 g) all-purpose flour

1 tablespoon (8 g) cornstarch

1 teaspoon kosher salt

½ teaspoon ground black pepper

1 cup (240 ml) light beer (such as a lager or pale ale)

FOR TACOS

1½ pounds (681 g) whitefish fillets, cut into 4 × 1-inch (10 × 2.5 cm) strips

Salt and ground black pepper

12 (5-inch, or 13 cm) tortillas, warmed

2 cups (140 g) finely shredded cabbage

Chopped fresh cilantro for garnishing

Pico de gallo for serving

Salsa verde for serving

Lime wedges for serving

INSTRUCTIONS

Pour the oil into a large deep skillet to a depth of 1 inch (2.5 cm). Heat the oil until a deep-fat thermometer registers 360°F (182°C), or the end of a wooden spoon sizzles when dipped into the hot oil.

To make the Baja sauce: In a small bowl, stir together all of the ingredients until smooth. Set aside until ready to use.

To make the beer batter: In a wide shallow bowl, combine the flour, cornstarch, salt, and pepper. While whisking, gradually pour in the beer until smooth and well-blended.

To make the tacos: Season the fish all over with salt and pepper. Working in batches, dip the fish into the beer batter and coat evenly on all sides. Fry in the hot oil for about 2 minutes per side until golden brown and cooked through, when it flakes easily with a fork. Transfer to paper towels to drain.

Arrange the tortillas on plates and spread a couple spoonfuls of Baja sauce down the center of each. Top with equal portions of fish, cabbage, and cilantro. Serve with pico de gallo, salsa verde, and lime wedges on the side.

RECIPE NOTE

Adobo sauce can be found in the Hispanic aisle of well-stocked supermarkets. Chipotle chiles are often sold canned in adobo sauce, and you can simply use this sauce for the recipe.

ISLE ROYALE NATIONAL PARK

THOMAS JEFFERSON'S VANILLA ICE CREAM

For me, sweet treats like ice cream and pie go hand in hand with national parks. Few visits end without a sugar cone heaped high with a creamy scoop of ice cream or a souvenir pie to bring back to camp.

Clearly, I'm not alone in my cravings, as ice cream can be found in almost every national park concessioner across the country, and none may be more famous than "TJ's Ice Cream" at Mt. Rushmore National Memorial—that's Thomas Jefferson, mind you, principal author of the Declaration of Independence and . . . the first ice cream recipe in the country?!

Apparently the process for making ice cream was not self-evident, so the U.S. president actually *wrote down* the first American ice cream recipe in 1780. Although he didn't invent ice cream, it certainly became more popular during his presidency and he is credited with being the first person to put the process into words—one of only ten recipes surviving in Jefferson's hand, and which is now safely stored in the Library of Congress. The recipe is believed to date from his time in France and originate from his French butler, Adrien Petit.

The president's namesake ice cream at Mt. Rushmore—full of rich, old-fashioned vanilla flavor—is based on his original recipe and here it is, slightly condensed. (You'll find a modern version of these instructions on the opposite page.)

INGREDIENTS

2 bottles of good cream

6 yolks of eggs

½ lb. sugar

INSTRUCTIONS

Mix the yolks & sugar. Put the cream on a fire in a casserole, first putting in a stick of Vanilla. When near boiling take it off & pour it gently into the mixture of eggs & sugar. Stir it well. Put it on the fire again stirring it thoroughly with a spoon to prevent it's sticking to the casserole. When near boiling take it off and strain it thro' a towel. Put it in the Sabottiere [the canister inside the pail] then set it in ice an hour before it is to be served. Put into the ice a handful of salt. Put salt on the coverlid of the Sabottiere & cover the whole with ice. Leave it still half a quarter of an hour.

Turn the Sabottiere in the ice 10 minutes. Open it to loosen with a spatula the ice from the inner sides of the Sabottiere. Shut it & replace it in the ice. Open it from time to time to detach the ice from the sides. When well taken (prise) stir it well with the Spatula.

Put it in moulds, justling it well down on the knee. Then, put the mould into the same bucket of ice. Leave it there to the moment of serving it. To withdraw it, immerse the mould in warm water, turning it well till it will come out & turn it into a plate.

VANILLA ICE CREAM (INSPIRED BY THOMAS JEFFERSON)

MAKES 2¼ QUARTS (2.4 L)

INGREDIENTS

2 quarts (1.9 L) heavy whipping cream

1 cup (200 g) sugar

1 vanilla bean

6 egg yolks

INSTRUCTIONS

In a large saucepan over medium heat, combine the heavy cream and sugar. Halve the vanilla bean lengthwise and scrape the seeds into the pan, then add the empty bean. Heat the mixture until bubbles form around the sides of the pan, stirring to dissolve the sugar but do not let the mixture boil. Remove from the heat and discard the bean.

In a large bowl, whisk the egg yolks. Temper the yolks by pouring in the hot cream mixture, a little at a time, and whisking it into the yolks until all of the hot cream is added to the bowl. The resulting custard should be smooth and well blended.

Pour the custard into the saucepan and cook over low heat, stirring constantly, for about 5 minutes until the mixture is thick enough to coat the back of a spoon and the temperature reaches 160°F (71°C). Transfer the custard to a large bowl and let cool at room temperature. Cover and refrigerate for several hours, or overnight.

Once the custard is very cold, pour it into the cylinder of your ice cream maker, up to two-thirds full, and churn following the manufacturer's instructions. Refrigerate the remaining custard until ready to freeze. Transfer the ice cream to a freezer-proof container and freeze for 4 to 6 hours, or until firm. Repeat with the remaining custard.

SUGAR CREAM PIE

Somewhere along your journey to Indiana Dunes, you've likely encountered the state pie of Indiana, a simple confection called sugar cream pie—or Hoosier pie. The silky, custard-like filling has a rich flavor reminiscent of crème brûlée, but this pie wasn't born of indulgence—it was known as "desperation pie," a pie made when times were tough and fresh fruit wasn't available. History traces its origins to the 1800s when Amish and Shaker settlers created sugar cream pies out of seasonal "desperation" with their waning provisions.

These days, sugar cream pies are a regional staple. If you can't take a drive on the Hoosier Pie Trail, which takes you to some of the best bakeries and restaurants serving this classic Indiana treat, you can easily make your own at home.

========== MAKES EIGHT SERVINGS ==========

INGREDIENTS

1 frozen premade pie shell, thawed

½ cup (100 g) granulated sugar

½ cup (112.5 g) brown sugar

2 tablespoons (15 g) all-purpose flour

2 cups (480 ml) heavy cream

2 teaspoons vanilla extract

Scant ½ teaspoon ground cinnamon

Scant ¼ teaspoon ground nutmeg

Powdered sugar for dusting

INSTRUCTIONS

Preheat the oven to 425°F (220°C or gas mark 7).

Prick the bottom and sides of the pie shell thoroughly with a fork. Place the shell on a sheet pan to catch any overspills.

In a medium-size bowl, combine the granulated sugar, brown sugar, and flour. Whisk in the heavy cream and vanilla until smooth. Pour the mixture into the prepared pie shell and sprinkle with cinnamon and nutmeg. Bake for 10 minutes.

Reduce the oven to 350°F (180°C or gas mark 4), then continue baking for 50 to 55 minutes. There should be lively boiling in the center of the pie, and more gentle bubbling on the edges where the filling has set.

Transfer the pie to a wire rack and let cool completely. Dust with powdered sugar and serve chilled or at room temperature.

AT-HOME TIP

I use a frozen pie shell for ease of prep, but you can certainly use your favorite homemade or store-bought piecrust for this recipe. Or, switch things up and try a graham cracker crust—it's delicious all ways.

INDIANA DUNES
NATIONAL PARK

PRICKLY PEAR AGUA FRESCA

Did you know cacti can be found as far north as Indiana? Eastern prickly pear, the state's only native cactus, grows along the trails of Indiana Dunes, where it thrives in the sandy soil and sunshine of the Lake Michigan shoreline. By late summer, the fat cactus pads of the prickly pear are adorned with ripe, edible fruits that make their way into markets until early fall.

Depending on the species, prickly pear fruits come in all shades of yellow, orange, green, red, and purple with varying degrees of sweetness and tartness. They're often turned into lemonade, but my favorite way to enjoy their full flavor is in an agua fresca—literally, "fresh water."

MAKES SIX TO EIGHT SERVINGS

INGREDIENTS

6 prickly pear cactus fruits, ends trimmed

6 cups (1.4 L) water, divided

½ cup (100 g) sugar, plus more as needed

1 lime wedge (optional)

Chili-lime salt for rimming the glass (optional)

INSTRUCTIONS

Peel the prickly pear by slicing ¼ inch (0.6 cm) through the skin from one end to the other lengthwise, then remove the whole peel with your fingers. It should come off easily in one piece and leave the flesh intact. Repeat with the remaining prickly pears and discard the peels.

In a blender, combine the prickly pears, 2 cups (480 ml) of water, and sugar. Blend for 30 seconds until the fruits are liquefied. Strain the juice through a fine-mesh sieve into a large pitcher. Stir in the remaining 4 cups (960 ml) of water. Taste and add more sugar, if desired. Chill and serve over ice.

Optionally, juice the lime wedge and use the rind to wet the rim of a glass. Pour the chili-lime salt onto a plate and gently press the wet rim of the glass into the salt. Add ice and serve the agua fresca in the prepared glass.

INDIANA DUNES NATIONAL PARK

FRUITED OATMEAL SOUP

Amidst 33,000 acres (13,355 ha) of parkland in Cuyahoga Valley and adjacent to Brandywine Falls is an elegant country inn that's easily mistaken for someone's house. Step inside the cozy Inn at Brandywine Falls and you'll feel like you're at a good friend's house—a friend who urges you to sit down to a hot bowl of oatmeal and a generous handful of Karen's Bird Seed (page 141) to hear about your week. For every guest, the nourishing breakfast is a highlight of their stay.

=== MAKES FOUR SERVINGS ===

INGREDIENTS

2 cups (480 ml) water

2/3 cup (96 g) Bob's Red Mill Scottish Stone Ground Oats

2/3 cup (80 g) Bob's Red Mill Oat Bran

1/4 cup (60 g) Greek yogurt

2 1/2 cups (600 ml) 2% milk

2 pears, peaches, or apples, peeled, cored, and chopped

INSTRUCTIONS

The night before serving, in a large microwavable bowl, stir together the water, oats, oat bran, and yogurt. Cover and let sit overnight.

The next day, add the milk and fruit to the bowl. Microwave on full power for 5 minutes. Stir until creamy and well blended. (Because microwaves vary, the oatmeal may require a few additional minutes of cooking time to reach a thick soup consistency.)

Serve with your favorite toppings, such as cinnamon, brown sugar, milk, yogurt, and/or Karen's Bird Seed (page 141).

RECIPE NOTE

If using peaches, top with fresh raspberries to serve. If using apples, soak some raisins or dried cranberries with the oats the night before. In winter, try soaking chopped dates or chopped dried apricots with the oats.

CUYAHOGA VALLEY
NATIONAL PARK

KAREN'S BIRD SEED

Guests at the Inn at Brandywine Falls *fly* through this granola and often ask for the recipe. It's named after the innkeeper's daughter-in-law (and creator of the delectable mix), but don't let that stop you from making it your own. This recipe lends itself to endless variations—feel free to experiment with add-ins like pecans or other nuts, chopped dried mango or other dried fruit, unsweetened coconut flakes (add these halfway through baking time), or spices and seasonings (try sea salt, cinnamon, ground ginger, or pumpkin spice blend).

MAKES 12 CUPS (1.5 KG)

INGREDIENTS

5 cups (400) rolled oats

1 cup (145 g) almonds

1 cup (100 g) walnuts

1 cup (168 g) flaxseed

¾ cup (112.5 g) sunflower seeds

½ cup (47 g) oat bran

½ cup (72 g) sesame seeds

⅔ cup (160 ml) vegetable oil

⅔ cup (227 g) blackstrap molasses

¾ cup (109 g) raisins

INSTRUCTIONS

Preheat the oven to 300°F (150°C or gas mark 2).

In a large bowl, combine the first seven ingredients.

In a small saucepan over medium-high heat, combine the oil and molasses and bring to a low boil. Pour the liquid over the oat mixture and stir well to coat every oat, nut, and seed. Spread the mixture across a large sheet pan in an even layer.

Bake for 1 hour, stirring every 20 minutes, until lightly browned on top.

Add the raisins while the mixture is hot. Stir every 20 minutes while the granola cools and crisps.

Once cooled, store the granola in an airtight container at room temperature, or in the refrigerator, for up to 2 weeks. For longer storage, freeze in a resealable zip-top bag and bring to room temperature before serving.

AT-HOME TIP

I recommend using a half-sheet pan or two quarter-sheet pans to toast the granola evenly in the oven.

CUYAHOGA VALLEY NATIONAL PARK

KENTUCKY BOURBON BALLS

A subterranean adventure at Mammoth Cave National Park, home of the world's longest-known cave system with more than four hundred miles (644 km) mapped and explored to date, is likely to end in one thing: a post-spelunking sipping tour on the Kentucky Bourbon Trail, where the state's historic distilleries have been producing the distinctive corn-based, barrel-aged whiskey since the 1780s.

But if you find it hard to drink your bourbon neat, there's an easier way to enjoy America's signature spirit and get all that great bourbon flavor, but none of the burn: Kentucky bourbon balls. The no-bake bite-size Southern confection was invented in 1938 by Ruth Hanly Booe of Rebecca Ruth Candies (known today as Rebecca Ruth Chocolates). After two years of perfecting her recipe, Ruth unveiled her boozy candy and they became such a hit that Kentucky is now synonymous with bourbon balls.

Although the original recipe is still a secret, you'll find that bourbon balls are as unique as their star ingredient, with every Kentucky household having their own way of making them. Following are three different ways you can coat your batch, but feel free to add your own flair for a holiday spread or your next Derby party.

===== **MAKES ABOUT FORTY BALLS** =====

INGREDIENTS

FOR BOURBON BALLS

1 cup (100 g) pecans, toasted and finely chopped

⅓ cup (80 ml) bourbon (100-proof Kentucky bourbon preferred)

8 tablespoons (1 stick, or 112 g) butter, at room temperature

3½ cups (392 g) powdered sugar

FOR COATING VARIATION 1

2½ cups (425 g) semisweet chocolate chips

2 tablespoons (28 g) coconut oil

⅓ cup (34 g) pecans, toasted and finely chopped

FOR COATING VARIATION 2

1½ cups (168 g) powdered sugar

FOR COATING VARIATION 3

¾ cup (84 g) powdered sugar

¾ cup (66 g) unsweetened cocoa powder

recipe continues

MAMMOTH CAVE NATIONAL PARK

INSTRUCTIONS

To make the bourbon balls: In a small shallow dish, combine the pecans and bourbon and soak overnight, stirring occasionally to make sure all the pecans are evenly soaked.

In the bowl of a stand mixer fitted with a paddle attachment, or in a large bowl and using a handheld electric mixer, beat the butter on medium speed until creamy. Gradually add the powdered sugar and continue beating until the mixture is dry and crumbly. Add the soaked pecans and any remaining bourbon and beat for a few seconds on low speed until well incorporated. Refrigerate the mixture for 1 hour.

Meanwhile, line two half-sheet pans with parchment paper and set aside. Once the mixture is chilled, using a small cookie scoop, scoop 1-inch (2.5 cm) balls and arrange them on the prepared sheet pans. Freeze for 1 hour until firm.

To coat the bourbon balls using coating variation 1: In a medium-size microwave-safe bowl, combine the chocolate and coconut oil. Microwave on full power for 1½ minutes until mostly melted, stopping and stirring at 30-second intervals. Be careful not to overheat the chocolate, which makes it thick, chunky, and dry. Once the chocolate is mostly melted, continue stirring and the last few pieces will melt completely.

Remove the first pan of bourbon balls from the freezer and, working one at a time, poke a toothpick into each ball and dip it into the melted chocolate. Use a spoon, as needed, to coat the ball evenly on all sides. Let any excess chocolate drip into the bowl, then return the coated ball to the pan, remove the toothpick, and

sprinkle some pecans on top. Repeat the process with the remaining balls. Let the chocolate harden before serving. To speed the process, place the pans of coated bourbon balls in the refrigerator.

To coat the bourbon balls using coating variation 2: Spread the powdered sugar across a small shallow dish and roll each ball in the sugar until evenly coated.

To coat the bourbon balls using coating variation 3: In a small shallow dish, stir together the powdered sugar and cocoa powder. Roll each ball in the mixture until evenly coated.

AT-HOME TIP

Bourbon balls can be made ahead and refrigerated in an airtight container for up to 3 weeks. You can also make the bourbon balls up to 2 months ahead and freeze them, then coat the frozen balls a few hours before serving.

WEST VIRGINIA SOUP BEANS AND CAST-IRON CORN BREAD

A visit to New River Gorge isn't complete without an iconic Southern meal of soup beans and corn bread to feed your belly and your soul. This is a dish that dates back to the coal mining days, when soup beans and corn bread were an affordable and practical source of sustenance for mountain folk throughout the Southern Appalachian region.

Despite the name, soup beans aren't soup; they're a steamy pot of brown beans, slowly simmered in a rich, creamy pot likker, and they only get better the longer they sit. Serve them with a crumbly wedge of corn bread for a warming winter meal.

MAKES SIX SERVINGS

INGREDIENTS

FOR BROWN BEANS

1 pound (454 g) dried pinto beans

1½ pounds (681 g) smoked ham hocks

1 yellow onion, quartered

6 garlic cloves, smashed with the flat side of a knife

4 thyme sprigs

2 bay leaves

1½ teaspoons kosher salt, plus more to taste

Ground black pepper

FOR CORN BREAD

2 eggs

1 (14-ounce, or 395 g) can cream-style sweet corn

½ cup (120 ml) milk

½ cup (120 g) sour cream

⅓ cup (80 ml) olive oil

1½ cups (210 g) yellow cornmeal

1 tablespoon (14 g) baking powder

2 teaspoons kosher salt

1 cup (100 g) chopped scallions

1 cup (115 g) shredded pepper Jack cheese

1 jalapeño pepper, minced

4 bacon slices

INSTRUCTIONS

To make the brown beans: Place the beans in a Dutch oven and add water until it rises about 2 inches (5 cm) above the level of the beans. Cover, bring to a boil, then remove from the heat and let soak for 1 hour.

Add the ham hocks, onion, garlic, thyme, bay leaves, and salt and stir to combine. Bring to a boil, then reduce the heat to maintain a simmer and cook, uncovered, for up to 2 hours, depending on your preferred level of tenderness. (Softer beans may require a longer cooking time.) Start checking the beans at the 1-hour mark, adding more water, as needed, to keep the beans submerged.

Once the beans are cooked to your liking, remove the meat from the bones and discard the fat and bones. Coarsely chop the meat and stir it into the beans. Season with salt and pepper to taste. Discard the thyme sprigs and bay leaves before serving.

recipe continues

NEW RIVER GORGE NATIONAL PARK

To make the corn bread: Preheat the oven to 400°F (200°C or gas mark 6).

In a large bowl, whisk the eggs, corn, milk, sour cream, and oil to blend. Stir in the cornmeal, baking powder, and salt until combined, then mix in the scallions, cheese, and jalapeño.

In a 10-inch (25 cm) cast-iron skillet over medium heat, fry the bacon until crisp. Reserve 1 tablespoon (15 ml) of bacon fat in the skillet and transfer the bacon to a cutting board. Finely chop the bacon and stir it into the cornmeal batter.

Swirl the bacon fat in the skillet to evenly coat the bottom. Pour the batter into the skillet and smooth the top with a rubber spatula. Bake for about 30 minutes until the edges are golden brown and a toothpick inserted into the center comes out clean.

Let rest for 15 minutes before slicing and serving with a bowl of soup beans.

VIRGINIA PEANUT SOUP

When I first came across peanut soup at Big Meadows Lodge in Shenandoah National Park, I was curious to try it but felt like I was rolling the dice on a pretty peculiar-sounding dish. As it turns out, the creamy colonial-era soup is not only a signature of the Spottswood Dining Room, but a Virginia classic since the early 1700s.

Peanuts arrived in Virginia via the slave trade, intended as food for the poor and eaten by enslaved Africans during their passage to the New World. The slaves brought and adapted many of the recipes from their homeland, shaping the Southern cuisine we know today, and peanut soup was one of them. With its reputation as slave food and animal feed, however, peanuts didn't take off until after the Civil War, when Confederate soldiers introduced their Union counterparts to the legume. As peanuts and peanut butter became more widely available during the twentieth century, so did peanut soup, which started appearing in cookbooks and newspapers and, ironically, the menus of swank local restaurants.

The simple dish straddles the line between sophisticated and plain. It's made many different ways from thin and brothy to thick and more bisque-like, and my version is the latter. I love the sweetness that sweet potatoes and coconut milk add, but not in a cloying way. This is a stick-to-your-ribs type of soup and one worth trying if you love traditional comfort foods with a rich history. Don't skip the lime juice before serving —it really brings out all the flavors.

━━━ MAKES SIX SERVINGS ━━━

INGREDIENTS

4 tablespoons (½ stick, or 56 g) butter

2 celery stalks, diced

1 yellow onion, diced

1 sweet potato, peeled and diced

3 tablespoons (22.5 g) all-purpose flour

6 cups (1.4 L) chicken broth

1 (15-ounce, or 44 ml) can coconut milk

1½ cups (390 g) creamy natural peanut butter, well-stirred

1 tablespoon (15 ml) sriracha

Salt and ground black pepper

Chopped salted peanuts for garnishing

Sliced scallions for garnishing

Lime wedges for serving

INSTRUCTIONS

In a medium-size stockpot over medium heat, melt the butter. Add the celery, onion, and sweet potato and cook for about 10 minutes until tender, stirring occasionally. Sprinkle the flour over the vegetables and stir to coat. Pour in the broth and coconut milk, increase the heat to high, and bring to a boil, stirring frequently. Reduce the heat to maintain a simmer and cook for 20 minutes until the vegetables are softened.

Remove from the heat and use an immersion blender to puree the mixture until smooth (or transfer, in batches, to a standard blender and return the pureed soup to the pot).

Whisk in the peanut butter and sriracha. Warm over low heat for about 5 minutes, whisking often. Season with salt and pepper to taste, as needed.

Garnish the soup with a handful of peanuts and scallions and squeeze some lime juice into each bowl before serving.

SHENANDOAH NATIONAL PARK

AT-HOME TIP

To prevent the cornstarch from clumping as you whisk it into the compote, use a fine-mesh sieve to sift the cornstarch into the hot syrup.

MILE-HIGH BLACKBERRY ICE CREAM PIE

The finest views of Shenandoah National Park can be found on Skyline Drive, a 105-mile (169 km) winding road that runs along the crest of the Blue Ridge Mountains through the length of the park.

At its highest point at 3,680 feet (5,922 km) stands Skyland, a historic resort that opened in the late 1800s as a summer retreat for weary urbanites. This is where you can relax after a hard hike and enjoy a meal with a view in the Pollock Dining Room. Considering the elevation of Skyland, it's only fitting that the house specialty is their Mile-High Blackberry Ice Cream Pie, famous for its pillowy meringue topping.

━━━ MAKES EIGHT SERVINGS ━━━

INGREDIENTS

FOR ICE CREAM LAYER

1 premade graham cracker piecrust

½ gallon (1.9 L) blackberry ice cream, slightly softened

FOR MERINGUE

4 egg whites, at room temperature (see Recipe Note)

½ cup (100 g) sugar

½ teaspoon kosher salt

½ teaspoon vanilla extract

FOR COMPOTE

2 cups (290 g) fresh blackberries

¼ cup (60 ml) freshly squeezed orange juice

1½ cups (300 g) sugar

2 tablespoons (30 ml) freshly squeezed lemon juice

2 tablespoons (16 g) cornstarch

Fresh blackberries for garnishing

INSTRUCTIONS

Optional step: Preheat the oven to 375°F (190°C or gas mark 5).

Before you begin making the pie, bake the graham cracker piecrust for 6 to 8 minutes. This step isn't necessary, but baking the crust crisps it up and deepens the flavor. If you bake the crust, make sure it cools completely before assembling the pie.

To make the ice cream layer: Scoop the ice cream into the cold crust and smooth the top. Freeze for about 3 hours until the ice cream is very hard.

To make the meringue: In the bowl of a stand mixer fitted with a whisk attachment, or in a large bowl and using a handheld electric mixer, beat all the ingredients on high speed for about 3 minutes until soft peaks form. Spread the meringue over the ice cream, swirling the meringue into decorative peaks with the back of a large spoon. Return the pie to the freezer and leave overnight.

To make the compote: In a medium-size saucepan over medium-low heat, combine the blackberries, orange juice, sugar, and lemon juice. Cook for 6 to 8 minutes until the blackberries break down and the mixture has a syrupy consistency, stirring frequently to prevent sticking and burning. Gradually whisk in the cornstarch, a little at a time, until thickened.

Before serving, brown the meringue with a kitchen torch. Serve each slice with a drizzle of compote on top and garnish with a few blackberries.

RECIPE NOTE

Eggs are easier to separate when they're cold, then can be left out until they reach room temperature.

SHENANDOAH NATIONAL PARK

PIMENTO CHEESE

Affectionately referred to as "Carolina caviar" or "Southern pâté," pimento cheese has been a Southern staple for decades, though it started as a northern invention by food manufacturers. The first pimento cheese appeared in 1910 as a blend of Neufchâtel cheese and diced pimiento peppers—two products of industrial food processing that took off in a time when canned goods were considered fashionable for entertaining. Commercially made pimento cheese expanded in popularity to the Midwest and as far west as Oregon, eventually making its way south in the 1930s. Those who lived in "the country," or who couldn't afford it, made their own, giving way to the pimento cheese we know today.

Traditional Southern recipes sometimes omit the cream cheese, but I find it gives the condiment a nice consistency. Serve it with crackers or crudités, or use it as a spread for a more substantial deli-style sandwich to take with you on your trek through Congaree National Park.

===== MAKES 2 CUPS (496 G) =====

INGREDIENTS

2 cups (230 g) shredded extra-sharp cheddar cheese

8 ounces (225 g) cream cheese, cut into 1-inch (2.5 cm) cubes, at room temperature

¼ cup (56 g) mayonnaise

¼ teaspoon garlic powder

¼ teaspoon onion powder

¼ teaspoon cayenne pepper (optional; omit if sensitive to spice)

1 (4-ounce, or 115 g) jar diced pimientos, drained (see Recipe Note)

1 jalapeño pepper, minced (optional; omit if sensitive to spice)

Salt and ground black pepper

INSTRUCTIONS

In a food processor, combine the cheddar, cream cheese, mayonnaise, garlic powder, onion powder, and cayenne (if using) and process until smooth. Add the pimientos and jalapeño (if using) and pulse until just combined. Transfer to a serving bowl and stir in a few pinches of salt and pepper to taste.

Serve immediately, or refrigerate in an airtight container for up to 1 week. Bring to room temperature before serving.

RECIPE NOTE

Pimiento peppers can be found in well-stocked supermarkets near the jars of roasted red peppers. If you can't find pimientos, substitute ½ cup (100 g) finely chopped roasted red peppers.

Pimento cheese is made with pimiento peppers—so where did the "i" go? When the Spanish sweet peppers started being canned and sold in the 1890s, it introduced the Spanish word *pimiento* to the American food market. By the turn of the century, however, most print accounts of the peppers called them pimentos (for some unknown reason). Today, they're known by both names, though purists insist on calling them pimientos.

CONGAREE
NATIONAL PARK

FROGMORE STEW

There are no restaurants in Congaree National Park, and after a day of hiking through floodplain forests or canoeing on Cedar Creek, your stomach will be rumbling for a taste of the region's famous low-country cooking. Luckily, it's an easy drive to the coastal plains, where you can sit down to a newspaper-covered table piled high with the local seafood boil known as Frogmore stew.

Despite its name, the dish does not contain frogs, nor is it even a stew. Frogmore stew originated in the small low-country fishing community of Frogmore on St. Helena Island off the South Carolina coast. It's a crowd-pleaser that can scale up to feed the entire block, and it's super adaptable to whatever you have in the kitchen. Don't be afraid to dump in some crab, clams, scallops, or fish, if you'd like! (Just be sure to adjust the cooking times for each type of seafood.)

AT-HOME TIP

For more flavor, boil the stew in light beer or chicken broth (or a half-and-half mixture with water).

INGREDIENTS

14 cups (3.3L) water

3 tablespoons (21 g) Old Bay Seasoning, plus more for serving

1 teaspoon kosher salt

1½ pounds (681 g) baby red potatoes

4 links (about 14 ounces, or 395 g) hot smoked sausage, cut into 2-inch (5 cm) pieces

3 ears corn, husked, cobs halved

2 pounds (908 g) peel-on shrimp

Melted butter for serving

Cocktail sauce for serving (optional)

Tartar sauce for serving (optional)

INSTRUCTIONS

In a large stockpot over high heat, combine the water, Old Bay, and salt and bring to a boil. Add the potatoes and cook for 15 minutes. Add the sausage and cook for 5 minutes. Add the corn and cook for 5 minutes. Stir in the shrimp and cook for 3 to 4 minutes until pink. Strain and transfer to a large platter, individual plates, or a newspaper-lined table for serving.

Serve with melted butter and additional Old Bay for seasoning, and cocktail sauce (if using) and tartar sauce (if using) for dipping.

CONGAREE
NATIONAL PARK

CONCH FRITTERS WITH KEY LIME AIOLI

Although every national park is unique, Biscayne may be the *most* unique, as 95 percent of the park is underwater! Biscayne is the largest marine park in the country, encompassing the northernmost section of the Florida Keys. With a snorkel or some diving gear, you might luck upon the famous pink-lipped conch shells the islands are known for. Although conchs in Biscayne are protected, they're found throughout the Caribbean and dominate menus as the local specialty. Because of that, conch fritters taste like vacation to me! (A vacation I try to replicate at home.)

MAKES TWENTY TO TWENTY-FOUR FRITTERS

INGREDIENTS

FOR AIOLI

1 cup (224 g) mayonnaise

2 tablespoons (30 ml) freshly squeezed key lime juice

2 teaspoons hot sauce

½ teaspoon grated key lime zest

½ teaspoon kosher salt

FOR FRITTERS

Vegetable oil for frying

1¼ cups (150 g) all-purpose flour

½ cup (120 ml) milk

1 egg

1 teaspoon baking powder

1 teaspoon Creole seasoning

1 cup (167 g) finely chopped conch meat, thawed if frozen

½ cup (80 g) finely chopped yellow onion

½ cup (75 g) finely chopped bell pepper

½ cup (60 g) finely chopped celery

½ Scotch bonnet pepper, minced

INSTRUCTIONS

To make the aioli: In a small bowl, stir together all the ingredients and refrigerate until ready to serve.

To make the fritters: Pour the oil into a large deep skillet to a depth of 1 inch (2.5 cm). Heat the oil until a deep-fat thermometer registers 360°F (182°C), or the end of a wooden spoon sizzles when dipped into the hot oil.

Meanwhile, in a large bowl, stir together the flour, milk, egg, baking powder, and Creole seasoning until no dry pockets remain. Add the conch, onion, bell pepper, celery, and Scotch bonnet and stir to combine.

Working in batches, using two spoons or a small cookie scoop, scoop 1-inch (2.5 cm) balls of the conch mixture and gently drop them into the hot oil. Fry for 3 to 4 minutes until golden brown, turning frequently with tongs, so they fry evenly on all sides. Transfer the fritters to paper towels to drain, then serve immediately with the aioli.

RECIPE NOTE

Outside of southern Florida, frozen conch meat is available in most Caribbean and Latin American markets and specialty seafood markets. Occasionally, you can also find it in Asian supermarkets. Shrimp, clams, or lobster meat can be substituted in a pinch.

BISCAYNE NATIONAL PARK

AT-HOME TIP

If your conch meat doesn't come tenderized, you can tenderize it yourself by pounding it with a meat mallet until it resembles a chicken cutlet. Then, finely chop the meat by hand or in a food processor.

FRIED FISH AND FUNGI WITH CREOLE SAUCE

Considered the national dish of the U.S. Virgin Islands, fish and fungi is found in homes and restaurants on every island, and every family and chef has their own way of making it. Sometimes, the fish is steamed or fried, and sometimes it's also served with plantains or malanga (a taro-like root). If you want to stick with tradition, use small, whole red snapper—but my version calls for fillets, which are easier to find.

======= MAKES SIX SERVINGS =======

INGREDIENTS

FOR CREOLE SAUCE

¼ cup (60 ml) olive oil

2 yellow onions, cut into ¼-inch (0.6 cm) slices

1 red bell pepper, cut into ¼-inch (0.6 cm) slices

1 green bell pepper, cut into ¼-inch (0.6 cm) slices

4 garlic cloves, sliced

1 (14-ounce, or 395 g) can tomato sauce

1 tablespoon (15 ml) distilled white vinegar

1 tablespoon (12 g) Creole seasoning or other seasoning salt (such as Lawry's)

Salt and ground black pepper

FOR FISH

Vegetable oil for frying

¾ cup (90 g) all-purpose flour

1 tablespoon (12 g) Creole seasoning or other seasoning salt (such as Lawry's)

6 (6-ounce, or 170 g) red snapper fillets

Salt and ground black pepper

6 servings Fungi (page 160)

INSTRUCTIONS

To make the Creole sauce: Place a large saucepan over medium-high heat and drizzle in the oil. Add the onions, red bell pepper, green bell pepper, and garlic and cook for 5 to 7 minutes, stirring occasionally, until tender. Pour in the tomato sauce. Fill the empty can to the top with water and add the water to the pan. Bring to a boil.

Once boiling, stir in the vinegar and Creole seasoning. Season with salt and pepper to taste. Lower the heat to maintain a simmer, cover the pan, and simmer gently until ready to serve.

To make the fish: Pour the oil into a large deep skillet to a depth of 1 inch (2.5 cm). Heat the oil until a deep-fat thermometer registers 360°F (182°C), or the end of a wooden spoon sizzles when dipped into the hot oil.

Meanwhile, in a large shallow dish, whisk the flour and Creole seasoning to blend. Season the fish fillets with salt and pepper, then dip them into the flour mixture to coat evenly on both sides.

Working in batches, lay the fillets in the hot oil and fry for 3 to 4 minutes until golden brown. Gently flip the fillets over and fry for 2 to 3 minutes more until cooked through, when they flake easily with a fork. Transfer to paper towels to drain and cover loosely with aluminum foil to keep warm. Repeat with the remaining fillets.

Serve the fish with a generous heap of Creole sauce on top and a couple scoops of fungi on each plate. Serve additional Creole sauce with the fungi.

VIRGIN ISLANDS
NATIONAL PARK

FUNGI

Fungi (pronounced "foon-jee") doesn't refer to mushrooms here. It's the Caribbean version of polenta—just as thick and hearty, but with okra and, occasionally, other ingredients mixed in. Fungi is a comfort food for people on the islands and is often served with fish (in a national staple known as fish and fungi, see page 159) or with sautéed greens on top. For a lighter meal, serve it as a satisfying vegetarian main course. I like the extra creaminess that coconut milk adds, but you can skip it and use an equal amount of water to cook the fungi.

MAKES FOUR TO SIX SERVINGS

INGREDIENTS

1 tablespoon (15 ml) olive oil

1/4 cup (40 g) finely diced yellow onion

1/4 teaspoon chopped fresh thyme leaves

1 garlic clove, minced

1 cup (152 g) thinly sliced frozen okra

1/4 cup (37.5 g) finely diced red bell pepper

3 cups (720 ml) hot water, divided

1 (14-ounce, or 400 ml) can coconut milk

1 cup (140 g) fine-ground cornmeal

2 tablespoons (28 g) butter

1 teaspoon kosher salt

INSTRUCTIONS

Place a medium-size saucepan over medium-high heat and drizzle in the oil. Add the onion, thyme, and garlic and cook for about 1 minute until soft and translucent. Add the okra and bell pepper and cook for about 3 minutes until tender.

Add 2 cups (480 ml) of hot water and the coconut milk and bring to a boil, stirring occasionally.

While whisking constantly, gradually add the cornmeal to the boiling water-milk mixture, a little at a time to avoid lumps, until all the cornmeal is incorporated.

Reduce the heat to low and cook until the mixture thickens. Whisk in 1/2 cup (120 ml) of hot water, cover the pan, and cook for 10 minutes.

Add the butter and salt and whisk until creamy. If you prefer a softer texture, whisk in more hot water, 1/4 cup (60 ml) at a time, until the consistency is to your liking. You may not need all of the hot water. The fungi should be firm but not stiff. Once it breaks away easily from the sides of the saucepan, remove it from the heat.

To serve, wet the inside of four small bowls with water. Scoop the fungi into each bowl, press firmly, and smooth the top to form a mold. Let the fungi set for a few minutes, then invert each bowl onto a plate so the fungi falls out in a nicely shaped mound. Serve as is, or make an indentation on top with a spoon and heap in your choice of stew or sauce.

VIRGIN ISLANDS
NATIONAL PARK

4

NATIONAL PARKS OF ALASKA

THE LAST FRONTIER IS A LAND OF MANY EXTREMES: It's home to the highest mountain peak in North America (Denali), the largest national park in the United States (Wrangell–St. Elias), and the least visited national park in the National Park System (Gates of the Arctic).

When President Jimmy Carter designated more than forty-three million acres (17,401 ha) of Alaska as national parkland in the Alaska National Interest Lands Conservation Act (ANILCA), it doubled the size of the NPS in one fell swoop. The conservation effort wasn't without controversy, but over time, support for ANILCA has grown as the protected areas have become a boon to the local economy. More than three million people visit Alaska's national park sites every year, and despite the influx of tourists, much of the state remains wild and accessible only by boat or plane (or on foot, for the truly adventurous).

Kenai Fjords National Park

Wrangell-St. Elias National Park

4

TRY THIS

Give the salmon patties an Asian twist by adding 2 teaspoons chili garlic paste, 2 teaspoons grated garlic, 2 teaspoons toasted sesame oil, and use lime juice in place of lemon juice. Serve the patties with an Asian-inspired salad and top with sweet chili sauce.

SALMON PATTIES

As the only fishing lodge and wilderness retreat on the shores of Crescent Lake, twenty river miles from Cook Inlet, Redoubt Mountain Lodge is perfectly situated for incredible fishing of all kinds in Lake Clark National Park. Sockeye, coho, king, and pink salmon abound in the glacier-fed waters and often make it back to the lodge, where Chef Sasha Kliman whips up a full feast of regional specialties for guests. This recipe is courtesy of her cookbook, *My Cabin Table*.

MAKES EIGHT PATTIES

INGREDIENTS

¼ cup (56 g) mayonnaise

2 tablespoons (30 ml) sriracha

1 tablespoon (15 ml) freshly squeezed lemon juice

1 teaspoon Dijon mustard

1 teaspoon Old Bay Seasoning

¾ teaspoon kosher salt

½ teaspoon Worcestershire sauce

¼ teaspoon ground black pepper

1¼ pounds (568 g) skinless salmon fillets, finely chopped into ¼-inch (0.6 cm) pieces

1¼ cups (62.5 g) panko bread crumbs, divided

⅓ cup (40 g) finely diced celery

¼ cup (25 g) thinly sliced scallions

2 tablespoons (8 g) finely chopped fresh parsley

2 tablespoons (8 g) finely chopped fresh dill

½ cup (120 ml) vegetable oil

Microgreens for serving

Tartar sauce, store-bought or homemade (see sidebar at right) for serving

Lemon wedges for serving

INSTRUCTIONS

In a large bowl, whisk the mayonnaise, sriracha, lemon juice, Dijon, Old Bay, salt, Worcestershire sauce, and pepper until smooth. Add the salmon, ¼ cup (12.5 g) of panko, celery, scallions, parsley, and dill and stir until just combined.

Pour the remaining 1 cup (50 g) of panko into a shallow dish. Scoop out a palm-size amount of the salmon mixture, shape it into a 3½-inch (8.5 cm) patty about 1 inch (2.5 cm) thick, and dip the patty in the panko until evenly coated on both sides. Repeat until you have eight panko-crusted patties.

In a large skillet over medium-high heat, heat the oil until shimmering. Working in batches, cook the patties for 2 to 3 minutes per side until golden brown and crispy. Transfer to paper towels to drain.

Serve the patties on a bed of microgreens with tartar sauce and lemon wedges on the side.

QUICK TARTAR SAUCE

Combine 1 cup (224 g) high-quality mayonnaise, such as Hellmann's or Duke's, 1½ tablespoons (23 g) sweet pickle relish, 1½ tablespoons (22.5 ml) freshly squeezed lemon juice, 1 tablespoon (10 g) minced red onion, 1 teaspoon Dijon mustard, and salt and pepper to taste.

LAKE CLARK NATIONAL PARK

LEMON GARLIC SALMON WITH GREMOLATA

For an angler, a day at Redoubt Mountain Lodge often entails a day on the water with their expert fishing guides. You might troll the lake, fish the lake fork of the Crescent River, jet boat the inlet rivers, or go on a fly-out (the ultimate Alaskan experience) for some of the best king salmon fishing in the state. These are the types of adventures that inspire the food made by Chef Sasha Kliman, who often creates menus around the fresh catch of the day. This recipe is a favorite at the lodge and shared from her book, *My Cabin Table*.

MAKES FOUR SERVINGS

INGREDIENTS

FOR GREMOLATA

½ red onion, finely chopped

Red wine vinegar for marinating

½ cup (32 g) chopped fresh parsley

¼ cup (60 ml) olive oil

½ teaspoon kosher salt

FOR SALMON

1½ pounds (681 g) salmon fillets

¼ cup (60 ml) olive oil

Grated zest of 2 lemons (refrigerate the lemons for another use if using the oven method; cut them into ¼-inch (0.6 cm)-thick slices if using the grill)

3 garlic cloves, minced

1 teaspoon paprika

1 teaspoon kosher salt

½ teaspoon ground black pepper

½ teaspoon red pepper flakes

INSTRUCTIONS

To make the gremolata: Place the onion in a medium-size bowl and add enough red wine vinegar to just barely cover the onion. Soak for at least 20 minutes.

In a small bowl, combine the parsley, oil, and salt. Strain the onion (save and store the vinegar for another use, if desired) and stir it into the parsley mixture.

To make the salmon (oven method): Preheat the oven to 400°F (200°C or gas mark 6). Line a large sheet pan with aluminum foil.

Pat the salmon dry with paper towels and place on the prepared sheet pan, skin-side down, if using fillets with skin on.

In a small bowl, whisk the oil, lemon zest, garlic, paprika, salt, pepper, and red pepper flakes to blend. Pour the mixture over the salmon, using a spoon to press the garlic and lemon zest into the flesh. Bake for about 15 minutes until the thickest part of the flesh registers 125°F (62°C). Remove from the heat and let rest for 5 minutes.

Serve the salmon with a few spoonfuls of gremolata on each fillet.

recipe continues

LAKE CLARK NATIONAL PARK

To make the salmon (grill method): Preheat the grill to medium-high heat (400°F to 425°F).

Pat the salmon dry with paper towels.

In a small bowl, whisk the oil, lemon zest, garlic, paprika, salt, pepper, and red pepper flakes to blend. Pour the oil mixture over the salmon, using a spoon to press the garlic and lemon zest into the flesh.

Arrange the lemon slices on the grill to create a "bed" for the salmon, slightly overlapping the slices.

Carefully place the salmon on top of the lemon slices, ensuring it does not touch the grate. Grill for about 15 minutes until the thickest part of the flesh registers 125°F (62°C), then remove from the heat and let rest for 5 minutes.

Serve the salmon with a few spoonfuls of gremolata on each fillet.

THE NATIONAL PARKS COOKBOOK

WILD GAME SAVORY CHEESECAKE WITH ALASKAN KING CRAB MUSTARD SAUCE

The family-owned Chulitna Lodge has a long history in Lake Clark, Alaska—decades before the wilderness area became a national park. Seven different families have owned the land since the first homesteaders arrived in 1932, and by the late 1970s, the Silber family made the property their summer vacation spot. Their son, Steve, now runs Chulitna Lodge as a wilderness retreat and artists' residence, giving his guests the full "bush luxury" experience, from the flight-seeing to the food. This recipe is a lodge favorite, courtesy of Steve Silber.

MAKES FOUR SERVINGS

INGREDIENTS

FOR ALASKAN KING CRAB MUSTARD SAUCE

1 tablespoon (15 ml) olive oil

½ cup (80 g) finely chopped yellow onion

½ cup (120 ml) chicken broth

½ cup (120 ml) heavy cream

2 tablespoons (30 g) brown mustard

1 teaspoon honey

1 teaspoon dried thyme

¼ teaspoon cayenne pepper

Alaskan king crabmeat, finely chopped (I recommend starting with ⅓ cup, or 45 g, and adding more as needed)

FOR CRUST

1 cup (115 g) bread crumbs

1 cup (100 g) grated parmesan cheese

½ cup (120 ml) melted butter

FOR FILLING

28 ounces (794 g) cream cheese, at room temperature

4 eggs

1 cup (120 g) shredded smoked Gouda cheese

½ cup (120 ml) heavy cream

2 tablespoons (30 ml) olive oil

1 yellow onion, diced

1 red bell pepper, diced

1 yellow bell pepper, diced

1 green bell pepper, diced

1 pound (454 g) moose sausage, finely diced

1 pound (454 g) Alaskan king crabmeat, coarsely chopped

2 teaspoons ancho chile powder

2 teaspoons chipotle powder

1 teaspoon kosher salt

½ teaspoon ground black pepper

recipe continues

LAKE CLARK
NATIONAL PARK

INSTRUCTIONS

To make the Alaskan king crab mustard sauce: In a medium-size saucepan over medium-high heat, heat the oil. Add the onion and cook for 2 to 3 minutes until translucent. Stir in the broth, heavy cream, brown sugar, mustard, honey, thyme, and cayenne. Add enough crabmeat to create your desired consistency and cook, stirring, until heated through. Set aside until ready to serve.

To make the crust: Preheat the oven to 400°F (200°C or gas mark 6).

In a medium-size bowl, combine the bread crumbs and parmesan. Stir in the melted butter until well incorporated. Press the mixture into a 10-inch (25 cm) springform pan and bake for 10 minutes.

To make the filling: Meanwhile, in a large bowl, whisk the cream cheese, eggs, Gouda, and heavy cream until combined.

In a large skillet over medium-high heat, heat the oil. Add the onion and all the bell peppers and cook for 6 to 8 minutes until soft. Add the sausage, crabmeat, ancho chile powder, chipotle powder, salt, and pepper and stir to coat the meats and vegetables thoroughly with the seasonings. Cook for about 5 minutes until the sausage is browned, then remove from the heat and let cool. Stir the cooled vegetables and meats into the cheese mixture until all the ingredients are combined.

To assemble the cheesecake: Reduce the oven temperature to 375°F (190°C or gas mark 5).

Pull out a sheet of heavy-duty aluminum foil (18 × 18 inches, or 45 × 45 cm) and center the springform pan on the foil. Tightly wrap the pan by bringing the foil up and crinkling it just under the edges of the pan all the way around. Repeat with a second sheet of foil to create a leakproof barrier for a water bath.

Place the wrapped springform pan in a baking dish large enough to hold the complete round. Add the cheesecake filling to the baked crust and cover the top of the pan with foil. Pour water into the baking dish until it reaches halfway up the sides of the pan. Bake the cheesecake in the water bath for 1½ hours. Increase the oven temperature to 450°F (230°C or gas mark 8) and bake for 15 minutes until the cheesecake is set and a knife inserted into the center comes out clean.

Remove the pan from the water bath and let cool, uncovered, on a wire rack.

To serve, unmold the sides of the pan from the cheesecake, slice the cake into wedges, and top each wedge with a few spoonfuls of Alaskan king crab mustard sauce. If desired, reheat the individual wedges and mustard sauce before serving.

RECIPE NOTE

No access to moose sausage? Substitute reindeer, elk, or your favorite beef sausage instead.

HALIBUT MARY JANE

Named for (and created by) Mary Jane Edney, this recipe has been served at Silver Salmon Creek Lodge for more than thirty years. The story began in 1991: Mary Jane and her daughter, Joanne, arrived on the beach in Lake Clark National Park for a deep-sea fishing excursion with David Coray, the owner of the lodge (and, unbeknownst to them at the time, Joanne's future husband). As they say . . . the rest is history. (Meanwhile, Mary Jane continued to fly into the Alaskan bush to fish until she was ninety-three years old!)

Today, David and Joanne regularly run world-class fishing trips deep into Cook Inlet in search of halibut, one of the staples at their lodge. This family recipe remains a favorite of their guests year after year.

=== MAKES SIX SERVINGS ===

INGREDIENTS

2 cups (480 g) sour cream

1¼ cups (280 g) mayonnaise

2 teaspoons freshly squeezed lemon juice

½ teaspoon garlic powder

½ teaspoon cayenne pepper, plus more as needed

½ teaspoon curry powder

½ teaspoon McCormick's Steak Seasoning, plus more as needed

2 to 2½ pounds (908 g to 1.1 kg) halibut fillets, cut into 2 × 1-inch (5 × 2.5 cm) strips

3 cups (216 g) crushed Ritz crackers

Nonstick cooking spray

¾ cup (86 g) shredded Gouda cheese

¼ cup (25 g) grated parmesan cheese

1 red bell pepper, thinly sliced

⅓ cup (37 g) chopped pecans

3 tablespoons (9 g) chopped fresh chives

INSTRUCTIONS

Preheat the oven to 450°F (230°C or gas mark 8).

In a medium-size bowl, stir together the sour cream, mayonnaise, lemon juice, garlic powder, cayenne, curry powder, and steak seasoning. Taste the mixture; it should be spicy and salty. If it tastes fairly mild, add more cayenne and steak seasoning (up to an additional teaspoon of each).

Pat the halibut dry with paper towels and stir the pieces into the sour cream mixture.

Spread the crushed crackers across a shallow dish and roll the halibut in the crackers to evenly coat all sides.

Lightly coat a sheet pan with cooking spray and arrange the halibut on the pan in a single layer. Sprinkle the Gouda and parmesan on top and garnish with the bell pepper, pecans, and chives.

Bake for 10 to 12 minutes until the thickest piece of fish is opaque white in the center. (Remember, it will continue to cook for a couple minutes after it's taken out of the oven.)

Pictured: Halibut Mary served with a quinoa and brown rice blend. (Silver Salmon Creek Lodge likes to serve theirs with wild rice.)

LAKE CLARK
NATIONAL PARK

RAZOR CLAM CHOWDER

The Cook Inlet coast of Lake Clark National Park experiences large tidal fluctuations, which temporarily expose the Pacific razor clam beds on the sandy beaches. Arguably one of the best-tasting clams, they can be harvested on minus tide cycles and there are usually a few good days every month.

When the tide is low, it's always fun to join the brown bears in an old-fashioned clam dig—all you need are mud-proof boots, a clam shovel or "clam gun," and a bucket of seawater. By the time your bucket is full of fresh razor clams, you're ready to warm up with this hearty chowder created by Chef Andrew Maxwell at Silver Salmon Creek Lodge. His suggestion: Serve it with a crusty slice of spruce tip sourdough bread and a cold beer.

MAKES TEN SERVINGS

INGREDIENTS

2 pounds (908 g) potatoes, peeled and cut into 1-inch (2.5 cm) cubes

8 ounces (225 g) bacon, cut into ½-inch (1 cm) pieces

1 tablespoon (15 ml) olive oil

1 pound (454 g) carrots, cut into 1-inch (2.5 cm) cubes

8 ounces (225 g) celery, diced

1 white onion, diced

4 garlic cloves, minced

1 teaspoon paprika

1 teaspoon sriracha

1 tablespoon (2 g) minced fresh rosemary leaves

1 tablespoon (2.5 g) minced fresh sage leaves

1 tablespoon (2.5 g) minced fresh thyme leaves

2 cups (480 ml) dry white wine

2 tablespoons (28 g) butter

3 tablespoons (22.5 g) all-purpose flour

4 cups (960 ml) milk

6 cups (1.4 L) chicken stock

1 cup (240 ml) heavy cream

½ teaspoon anchovy paste

1 pound (454 g) cleaned and chopped razor clams

Salt and ground black pepper

INSTRUCTIONS

Place the potatoes in a large pot and add enough water to cover by about 1 inch (2.5 cm). Bring to a boil, reduce the heat to a rapid simmer, and cook for 10 to 15 minutes until the potatoes are fork-tender. Drain and set aside.

Spread the bacon across a large cold skillet and place the skillet over medium-low heat to render the fat. Cook until the fat is mostly rendered but the bacon is not crispy, then drain on paper towels and set aside. Discard or reserve the bacon fat for another use.

In a large stockpot over medium heat, swirl in the oil and add the carrots, celery, and onion. Cook for 3 to 4 minutes until the onion is translucent. Stir in the garlic, paprika, and sriracha and cook for 1 to 2 minutes until the garlic is aromatic. Add the rosemary, sage, thyme, and wine and bring to a simmer. Cook until the wine is reduced to a few tablespoons (45 ml), stirring frequently.

Meanwhile, in a medium-size saucepan over medium heat, melt the butter. Stir in the flour and cook until lightly browned. Slowly add the milk, whisking vigorously to break up any lumps. Once the liquid has thickened, remove from the heat and set aside.

Check the stockpot with the vegetables; once the wine has reduced, pour in the stock and bring to a boil. Reduce the heat to maintain a simmer and cook until the carrots are tender. Stir in the thickened milk, heavy cream, and anchovy paste and return the chowder to a simmer. Add the clams, potatoes, and bacon. Taste the chowder and season with salt and pepper, as needed. Bring back to a simmer before serving.

LAKE CLARK
NATIONAL PARK

BEEF KOFTA WITH CHERMOULA

Travel ninety miles on Denali Park Road, a desolate, single-lane dirt road that cuts through the national park, and you'll find yourself at Camp Denali. As the only wilderness lodge inside the park, the end-of-the-road destination is unique for its stunning, up-close views of Denali and the Alaska Range. The remote location also means the lodge is far from supplies, a fact that both inspires and necessitates Camp Denali's commitment to sustainability. The lodge grows all of its own salad greens in an on-site greenhouse; sources grains, eggs, and other staples from Alaskan mills and farms; and serves 100 percent Alaskan meat, poultry, and seafood to its guests.

This recipe is just one example of Camp Denali's mission to support food purveyors across the state—from the grass-fed cow that's raised some three hundred miles (483 km) away to the fresh organic herbs and vegetables harvested from local farms and their own garden.

===== **MAKES TWELVE BROCHETTES** =====

INGREDIENTS

FOR CHERMOULA

1½ cups (24 g) packed fresh cilantro

1½ cups (90 g) packed fresh parsley

3 garlic cloves, peeled

2 tablespoons (30 ml) freshly squeezed lemon juice

1 tablespoon (7.5 g) paprika

1½ teaspoons cumin seeds, toasted

1½ teaspoons coriander seeds, toasted

½ teaspoon kosher salt

Pinch of cayenne pepper

⅓ cup (80 ml) olive oil

FOR KOFTA

2 pounds (908 g) ground beef

¾ cup (120 g) minced yellow onion, divided

⅓ cup (5 g) minced fresh cilantro

⅓ cup (20 g) minced fresh parsley

2 tablespoons (12 g) minced fresh mint

1½ teaspoons paprika

1½ teaspoons ground cumin

1½ teaspoons ground cinnamon

¾ teaspoon ground mace

½ teaspoon cayenne pepper

1½ teaspoons kosher salt

Olive oil (optional)

INSTRUCTIONS

To make the chermoula: In a food processor, combine all the ingredients, except the oil. Pulse until finely chopped and well combined, stopping to scrape down the sides of the bowl with a rubber spatula as necessary. With the motor running, slowly pour the oil through the feed tube until a smooth sauce forms. Transfer the chermoula to a bowl, cover, and set aside until needed.

recipe continues

DENALI
NATIONAL PARK

To make the kofta: In a large bowl, mix the ground beef, half the onion, and all the herbs and spices. Add the remaining onion as long as the mixture is not too moist; it should be a little sticky, like sausage. If the beef is relatively lean, add one to two swirls of olive oil, as needed.

Scoop a 3-ounce (85 g) portion of the beef mixture. Press it around a short skewer and then roll it on a cutting board or between your palms to form an even, sausage-shaped brochette about 4 inches (10 cm) long and 1 inch (2.5 cm) thick. Repeat with the remaining beef mixture until you have twelve skewers.

Preheat the grill to medium-high heat (about 400°F, or 200°C). Working in batches, if necessary, arrange the skewers on the grill grate and cook until the meat is firm to the touch and cooked through, about 4 minutes on the first side and 3 to 4 minutes on the second side.

Serve the kofta with chermoula on the side for dipping or drizzling.

Pictured: Beef kofta served on a bed of parsley, tomatoes, cucumber, and onion with pita and chermoula.

RAW STIRRED LINGONBERRIES

Alaska is well-known for its amazing and abundant wild berries in late summer—just ask any grizzly bear! And lingonberries, in particular, are a favorite forage among wildlife residents and human visitors in the Last Frontier. The tart red berries grow on short evergreen shrubs in the arctic tundra and boreal forests of Denali. Eager hikers can gather lingonberries by the bucketful or simply snack on them on the go. (Tip: They taste best after the first frost, which mellows their bite.)

If you don't have a trip to Denali planned anytime soon, you can use thawed frozen lingonberries to make this simple, traditional Scandinavian condiment. It's enjoyed as a sweet relish and can be spooned over Swedish pancakes, meatballs, oatmeal, or roasted meats like chicken and duck. Save the liquid from the stirred lingonberries to use in a Denali 75 cocktail (page 182).

===== **MAKES 1 CUP (ABOUT 250 G)** =====

INGREDIENTS

1 cup (150 g) lingonberries, thawed if frozen

½ cup (100 g) sugar

INSTRUCTIONS

In a small bowl, combine the lingonberries and sugar, mashing some with the back of a spoon to soften the berries. Let sit at room temperature for about 1 hour until the sugar dissolves, stirring occasionally. If not using right away, cover and refrigerate the lingonberries for up to 3 months.

DENALI
NATIONAL PARK

DENALI 75

The Denali 75 is my Alaskan twist on the French 75, a classic cocktail that's bubbly, citrusy, and refreshing. But don't let the dainty glasses fool you—it's made with a standard pour of gin *and* a sparkling wine float, so it definitely packs an effervescent punch. In fact, the original cocktail was named after the French 75-mm field gun, which was commonly used in World War I.

In this version, I use the liquid from my Raw Stirred Lingonberries (page 181) in place of simple syrup for a touch of sweetness and tartness. It's a favorite for any occasion that calls for a celebration.

INGREDIENTS

1½ ounces (45 ml) gin

¾ ounce (22.5 ml) lingonberry liquid from Raw Stirred Lingonberries (page 181)

¾ ounce (22.5 ml) freshly squeezed lemon juice

Dry sparkling wine (such as prosecco) for topping

Lingonberries for garnishing

Lemon twist for garnishing (optional)

INSTRUCTIONS

Fill a cocktail shaker with ice and pour in the gin, lingonberry liquid, and lemon juice. Cover and shake well, then strain into a champagne flute. Top with sparkling wine and garnish with a spoonful of lingonberries. Add a lemon twist (if using).

DENALI NATIONAL PARK

LINGONBERRY BRIE EN CROUTE

Lingonberries are found all over Southcentral Alaska, particularly in the tundra and mountain slopes of Denali. The tart red berries look like miniature cranberries (in fact, they're also known as lowbush cranberries), and though they're slightly sweeter, lingonberries are often used as a cranberry substitute.

One of my favorite ways to serve lingonberry sauce is over baked Brie—the kind of appetizer you need in your culinary repertoire if you want to serve something a little fancy, but don't want to spend a lot of time making it. And this baked Brie en croute (literally, "baked Brie in a pastry crust") is versatile enough to go from a cocktail party to a Thanksgiving dinner table, where the warmth of curry and the zest of lingonberries pair well with other autumn flavors.

=== **MAKES SIX TO EIGHT SERVINGS** ===

INGREDIENTS

1 cup (150 g) lingonberries, thawed if frozen

3 tablespoons (60 g) honey

1 tablespoon (15 ml) water, plus more as needed

1 teaspoon curry powder

All-purpose flour for dusting

1 puff pastry sheet (from a 17.3-ounce, or 490.5 g, package), thawed if frozen

1 (8-ounce, or 225 g) wheel Brie, rind intact

1 egg, beaten with 1 tablespoon (15 ml) water to make an egg wash

INSTRUCTIONS

Preheat the oven to 400°F (200°C or gas mark 6). Line a sheet pan with parchment paper.

In a small saucepan over medium heat, stir together the lingonberries, honey, water, and curry powder. Bring to a simmer and cook for 6 to 8 minutes, stirring occasionally, until the berries burst and soften. Add more water if needed, 1 tablespoon (15 ml) at a time, to keep the berries from sticking and burning. (My lingonberries release plenty of juices while they simmer, so I usually don't need more water.) Remove from the heat and let cool slightly to thicken the sauce.

Lightly dust a work surface with flour and unroll the puff pastry sheet on it. Using a rolling pin, roll the pastry dough into a 12-inch (30 cm) square and lay it flat on the prepared sheet pan. Center the Brie on the dough. Spread the lingonberry sauce evenly on top of the Brie. Fold the dough corners up and over the Brie, like you're wrapping a gift, pressing the dough together in the center and along the seams until the Brie is tightly wrapped. Brush the egg wash all over the top and sides of the dough.

Bake for 20 to 25 minutes until puffed and golden brown. Remove from the oven and let cool for 5 to 10 minutes. Transfer to a serving plate. Serve the baked Brie with crackers and dig in immediately to savor all the hot, gooey deliciousness.

DENALI
NATIONAL PARK

FORAGE AND FEAST ON THE BOUNTY OF THE NATIONAL PARKS

The prehistoric practice of foraging has exploded in recent years. At its most basic, foraging is the act of searching for and harvesting wild edibles such as flowers, fruits, fungi, nuts, seeds, vegetables, and a host of other foods found in nonagricultural settings. Although most people no longer forage for subsistence, many have probably joined in on a casual mushroom hunt or picked a handful of berries on a summer hike—activities that deepen our appreciation of nature and help us become more aware of our finite natural resources.

For the most part, removing, disturbing, or collecting any plants or parts of plants is prohibited in national parks, but the National Park Service leaves discretion up to the individual park superintendents. That means in more than half of America's national parks, foraging is not only allowed, but also encouraged, for personal enjoyment—within limits.

So, where can you legally harvest food in the wild? Here are thirteen places that let visitors sample some of their natural bounties.

Note that these regulations are current as of the time of writing, but always double-check with park rangers or consult the most recent superintendent's compendium (found online) before you harvest, as rules regarding the types and quantities of wild-harvested foods allowed may change from year to year.

ACADIA

Acadia allows foraging for personal consumption. You can harvest apples (limited to 10 dry gallons, weight varies, per person per day), other fruits and berries (up to 1 dry half-gallon, weight varies, per person per day), and nuts (up to 1 half-gallon, weight varies, per person per day). A "dry gallon" refers to a gallon of uncrushed berries and fruit.

DENALI

Berries abound in Denali in August and September, and the park places no limits on the amount of berries you can harvest—just that you harvest for personal consumption only. So, bring a bucket or an empty water bottle and fill it with your pick of blueberries (found in the Mountain Vista and Savage River areas) or lingonberries (found most easily on the trails around the Denali Visitor Center).

GLACIER

A hike on many of the trails around Glacier in mid- to late summer will bring you up close to several species of edible plants. The park allows hand gathering of up to 1 quart (weight varies) per person per day of chokecherries, gooseberries, huckleberries, serviceberries, and thimbleberries. (However tempting it may be, note that mushroom hunting is expressly prohibited.)

GREAT BASIN

The singleleaf pinyon pine is Nevada's state tree, and it's found abundantly in the park in mixed stands with Utah juniper between six-thousand- and nine-thousand-feet (1.8 and 2.7 km) elevations. In fall, gathering pine nuts from pinyon pine cones is a wonderful way to experience the natural bounty of Great Basin. A limit of twenty-five pounds (11.3 kg) per household (for personal noncommercial use) is allowed per year.

GREAT SMOKY MOUNTAINS

The Smokies have historically provided food for generations of homesteaders, and you can enjoy some of their wild bounties for yourself. Up to 1 pound (454 g) per person per day of edible mushrooms (of all fungal species) can be collected, as long as they're at least two hundred feet (61 m) from the trail. Up to 1 pound (454 g) per person per day of American hazelnuts, apples, blackberries, black raspberries, black walnuts, blueberries, cherries, currants, elderberries, gooseberries, grapes, hickory nuts, huckleberries, pawpaws, peaches, pears, persimmons, red mulberries, serviceberries, and strawberries (of each species) can be collected. Note that picking ramps and ginseng is expressly prohibited in the park.

HALEAKALĀ

Wild edibles are found all over the island of Maui, but within the park, you can pick akala berries (a native Hawaiian raspberry), kukui nuts, up to 1 quart (weight varies), and ohelo berries (a much-prized fruit related to cranberries), up to 1 quart (weight varies), per person per day for each.

ISLE ROYALE

Thimbleberries (see page 129) may be one of the more coveted things you can forage on Isle Royale, but the park is home to many more edible fruits, berries, and fungi that are legal to harvest. You can handpick 2 gallons (weight varies) of apples per person per day; 4 quarts (weight varies) of blueberries, mushrooms, raspberries, and thimbleberries per person per day; and 1 quart (weight varies) of beach peas, chokecherries, cranberries, currants, elderberries, hazelnuts, juneberries, pin cherries, rhubarb, rose hips, strawberries, and wintergreen berries per person per day.

MT. RAINIER

Mt. Rainier's diverse forest and subalpine ecosystems are home to dozens of edible mushroom species. From late summer to the first frost of fall, you can pick up to 1 gallon (weight varies) of edible fungi per person per day for personal consumption, including chanterelles, hedgehog mushrooms, hen-of-the-woods, matsutake, morels, pig's ear, and shaggy mane. The park also allows noncommercial picking of blackberries, blueberries, huckleberries, highbush cranberries, gooseberries, salmonberries, serviceberries, strawberries, and thimbleberries, up to 1 gallon (weight varies) per person per day.

ROCKY MOUNTAIN

If you need an on-the-go snack while hiking, Rocky Mountain allows handpicking of blueberries, chokecherries, raspberries, red elderberries, and strawberries, each limited to 1 quart (weight varies) per person per day (and only for personal consumption). Edible mushrooms are not permitted to be gathered.

SEQUOIA AND KINGS CANYON

These parks allow harvesting of watercress (leaves only), wild onions (tops only), and edible fungi, as long as they are cut, not pulled. You can also pick up to 1 pint (weight varies) per person per day (for immediate consumption only) of bilberries, blackberries, currants, elderberries, gooseberries, huckleberries, raspberries, strawberries, and thimbleberries.

Yosemite National Park

SHENANDOAH

Shenandoah is a forager's paradise and home to more than 1,400 species of plants. The park allows collection of up to 1 gallon (weight varies) per person per day of certain edible berries, fruits, and nuts, including American hazelnuts, blackberries, black walnuts, blueberries, cherries, currants, elderberries, gooseberries, grapes, hickory nuts, huckleberries, morel mushrooms, persimmons, plums, raspberries, serviceberries, strawberries, and wineberries. In addition, each person is allowed to collect up to 1 bushel (weight varies) per day of apples, peaches, and pears, and up to 1 quart (weight varies) per day (total combined volume) of all other edible fungi.

VIRGIN ISLANDS

If you love exotic fruits and want to try some new varieties, the Virgin Islands allows the handpicking of coconuts, genips, guavaberries, guavas, hog plums, limes, mamey apples, mangoes, papayas, sea grapes, soursop, sugar apples, and sweet limes. No limits are specified, just that you pick for personal use or consumption only.

YOSEMITE

Yosemite allows foragers to pick an unlimited quantity of Himalayan blackberries, as well as 1 pint (weight varies) per person per day (for immediate consumption only) of blackberries, edible fungi, elderberries, huckleberries, raspberries, strawberries, and thimbleberries. Note that all fungi must be cut (not pulled).

RUSSIAN RYE PANCAKE BREAKFAST

The first European explorers to reach Alaska were the Russians, and Chef Scott Neuse pays homage to those brave people by imagining what ingredients they would have brought with them when they arrived in the 1700s. This became his inspiration for the breakfast served at Kenai Fjords Wilderness Lodge, a secluded island getaway just off the eastern boundary of the national park.

First, you notice the heartiness and texture of the pancakes, which come from rye and wheat berries, long grown as the primary grain crops in Russia. Reindeer are found in both regions, and reindeer sausage is an especially beloved treat in Alaska—and makes a great accompaniment to these pancakes. Birch trees grow in boreal forests all over the state as well as the Russian territory, and the syrup has a strong flavor, similar to blackstrap molasses. This is a meal that's warmly familiar, but with an Alaskan bent.

INGREDIENTS

FOR BIRCH SYRUP BUTTER

1 cup (2 sticks, or 224 g) butter, at room temperature

2 tablespoons (36 g) birch syrup, real maple syrup (40 g), or molasses (40 g)

FOR SOFT BERRY COMPOTE

2 cups (290 g) mixed berries (such as strawberries and blueberries)

½ cup (100 g) granulated sugar

2 tablespoons (30 ml) water

2 teaspoons freshly squeezed lemon juice

1 teaspoon vanilla extract

1 tablespoon (7.5 g) all-purpose flour

FOR SWEETENED WHIPPED SOUR CREAM

¾ cup (180 ml) heavy cream

½ cup (120 g) sour cream

2 tablespoons (25 g) granulated sugar

½ teaspoon vanilla extract

FOR PANCAKES

1 cup (128 g) rye flour

½ cup (60 g) all-purpose flour

2 tablespoons (25 g) granulated sugar

1½ tablespoons (21 g) baking powder

Pinch of salt

1 egg

1½ tablespoons (22.5 ml) melted butter, cooled

½ teaspoon vanilla extract

1 cup (240 ml) milk, plus more as needed

⅓ cup (55 g) cooked wheat berries (optional)

Olive oil

Powdered sugar for serving

recipe continues

KENAI FJORDS NATIONAL PARK

INSTRUCTIONS

To make the birch syrup butter: In the bowl of a stand mixer fitted with a paddle attachment, or in a large bowl and using a handheld electric mixer, beat the butter and syrup until combined.

To make the soft berry compote: Coarsely chop any larger berries so all the fruit pieces are similar in size.

In a medium-size saucepan over medium heat, combine all the ingredients, except the flour, and cook until the berries start to release their juices. Mash the berries with a fork or spoon and stir occasionally to prevent them from sticking to the pan.

Once the berries are soft, spoon some of the hot juices into a small bowl and whisk in the flour to make a slurry. Add the slurry to the berries and cook for about 1 minute, whisking, until the mixture thickens. Remove from the heat.

To make the sweetened whipped sour cream: Put a mixing bowl in the freezer for a few minutes until cold, then add all the ingredients to the cold bowl. Using a handheld electric mixer or a whisk, beat for about 2 minutes until lightly whipped. Refrigerate until needed.

To make the pancakes: In a large bowl, whisk the rye flour, all-purpose flour, granulated sugar, baking powder, and salt to combine.

In a small bowl, whisk the egg, cooled butter, and vanilla. Add the wet ingredients to the dry ingredients and stir in the milk to make a lumpy batter. Add a little more milk, as needed, if the batter is too thick. The consistency should be thin and pourable. Stir in the wheat berries (if using).

Place a medium-size skillet over medium-low heat and drizzle in some oil. Pour about ¼ cup (58 g) of pancake batter in the center. Cook for 1½ to 2 minutes until bubbles have set along the edges of the pancake. Flip and cook for 1½ to 2 minutes more until firm and golden brown. Transfer the pancake to a warm oven or cover it loosely with aluminum foil to keep warm. Repeat with the remaining batter to make additional pancakes, adding more oil to the pan, as needed.

Serve dusted with powdered sugar and with the birch syrup butter, compote, and whipped sour cream on the side for topping.

BLUEBERRY AND SALMONBERRY FRANGIPANE TART

Guests at Kenai Fjords Wilderness Lodge are treated to a bumper crop of wild blueberries and salmonberries every summer on Fox Island, the blissfully remote locale just outside Kenai Fjords National Park. Most of the fruit gets eaten on the trails, but some make it into Chef Scott Neuse's berry-studded frangipane.

Salmonberries have a milder flavor than their raspberry cousins—tart and a tiny bit sweet, almost like rhubarb. They're found in the coastal regions of southern Alaska and are quite loved by both locals and visitors.

———— MAKES EIGHT SERVINGS ————

INGREDIENTS

FOR TART

1¼ cups (150 g) all-purpose flour, plus more for dusting

2 tablespoons (25 g) sugar

½ teaspoon kosher salt

7 tablespoons (98 g) cold butter, cut into small pieces

4 tablespoons (60 ml) ice-cold water

FOR FRANGIPANE

5 tablespoons (70 g) butter, at room temperature, plus more for the tart pan

⅓ cup (67 g) sugar

1 egg, at room temperature

½ teaspoon vanilla extract

½ teaspoon almond extract

1 teaspoon grated lemon zest

¾ cup (84 g) almond meal

2 tablespoons (15 g) all-purpose flour

Pinch of salt

2 cups (weight varies) blueberries, salmonberries, or raspberries (or a mix)

½ cup (46 g) sliced almonds (optional)

Powdered sugar for dusting

INSTRUCTIONS

To make the tart: In a food processor, combine the flour, sugar, and salt and pulse to combine. Add the butter and pulse until the mixture starts to resemble coarse sand.

Continue pulsing and add the water through the feed tube, starting with 2 tablespoons (30 ml) and adding 1 tablespoon (15 ml) at a time, up to 4 tablespoons (60 ml) total until the dough comes together. Do not overmix or the tart crust will not be flaky.

Shape the dough into a flat disk about 5 inches (13 cm) in diameter and wrap tightly in plastic wrap. Chill for at least 30 minutes in the refrigerator, or up to 2 days.

To make the frangipane: In the bowl of a stand mixer fitted with a paddle attachment, or in a large bowl and using a handheld electric mixer, cream together the butter and sugar on medium speed for 4 minutes. (Do not skip this step or your custard will not be as fluffy.) Reduce the speed to low, add the egg, and beat until fully incorporated. Beat in the vanilla, almond extract, and lemon zest. Continue beating on low speed and add the almond meal, flour, and salt.

KENAI FJORDS
NATIONAL PARK

Increase the speed to medium and beat for 4 to 5 minutes until the frangipane is very fluffy. Set aside until you're ready to assemble the tart. The frangipane can be made up to 1 day in advance and kept refrigerated.

To assemble the tart: Preheat the oven to 375°F (190°C or gas mark 5). Coat a round tart pan or 8-inch (20 cm) springform pan with butter.

Generously dust a work surface with flour. Remove the dough from the refrigerator and place it on the floured surface. Sprinkle a rolling pin with flour and roll out the dough from the center in all directions until it's about 11 inches (28 cm) in diameter. Place the dough in the prepared pan. You want the dough to come up about 1½ inches (3.5 cm) along the sides to form a well for the frangipane.

With a rubber spatula, spread the frangipane over the crust. Scatter the berries on top in a single layer and press very lightly into the frangipane. Add the sliced almonds (if using) evenly around the edges of the tart.

Place the tart in the freezer for 15 minutes. Once chilled, place the tart on a sheet pan and bake for 40 to 45 minutes until the frangipane is puffed around the berries. Remove from the oven and let cool on the sheet pan for 10 to 20 minutes. Remove the outer rim of the tart pan, dust the tart with powdered sugar, and serve warm or at room temperature.

WILD-CAUGHT COPPER RIVER RED SALMON WITH ONION GASTRIQUE

In the early 1900s, the former mining town of McCarthy, Alaska, was the largest city in the state. It's almost impossible to imagine these days, when you can walk the entire town in just a couple of minutes. But McCarthy is far from abandoned: It's the last remaining living community inside America's largest national park. It's also where the Salmon & Bear Restaurant at McCarthy Lodge—an unexpected foodie destination in the heart of Wrangell–St. Elias—serves an innovative menu of locally sourced and foraged ingredients, including the prized Copper River red salmon.

The fish, often touted as the "Wagyu of seafood," travel more than two hundred miles (322 km) from the ocean to their spawning grounds, packing on more omega-3 fats than other species of salmon while developing a succulent, buttery texture. The Copper River red salmon procured by McCarthy Lodge are unique in how they're harvested and cleaned, giving them a rich, full flavor. This recipe is adapted from one of Executive Chef Joshua Slaughter's signature dishes.

───── **MAKES FOUR SERVINGS** ─────

INGREDIENTS

FOR ONION GASTRIQUE

1 cup (240 ml) red wine vinegar

1 cup (200 g) sugar

2 white onions, thinly sliced

FOR DANDELION PISTOU

1 bunch dandelion greens, coarsely chopped

3 garlic cloves, peeled

Juice of 1 lemon

½ cup (120 ml) olive oil, plus more as needed

Salt and ground black pepper

FOR ROASTED POTATOES

1½ pounds (681 g) fingerling potatoes (Alaskan fingerlings preferred), halved lengthwise

Olive oil

Salt and ground black pepper

FOR FORAGED MUSHROOMS

2 tablespoons (30 ml) olive oil

12 ounces (340 g) wild mushrooms (morels preferred), cleaned and left whole or halved lengthwise, depending on the mushrooms

Salt and ground black pepper

FOR SALMON

4 (6-ounce, or 170 g) skin-on Copper River red salmon fillets

Salt and ground black pepper

Olive oil

Pineapple weed and wild sorrel for garnishing (optional)

recipe continues

WRANGELL-ST. ELIAS
NATIONAL PARK

INSTRUCTIONS

To make the onion gastrique: In a large saucepan over medium-high heat, combine the vinegar and sugar and cook, stirring, until the sugar dissolves. Stir in the onions and bring to a light boil. Cook for about 30 minutes until the onions are slightly translucent and the liquid has reduced and thickened, stirring occasionally. Keep warm until ready to serve.

To make the dandelion pistou: In a food processor, combine the dandelion greens, garlic, and lemon juice and process until well blended, stopping to scrape down the sides of the bowl with a rubber spatula, as needed. With the motor running, add a slow, steady stream of oil through the feed tube, starting with ½ cup (120 ml) and adding more, as needed (1 tablespoon, or 15 ml, at a time), to make a thick, sauce-like consistency. Season with salt and pepper to taste, then set aside.

To make the roasted potatoes: Preheat the oven to 425°F (220°C or gas mark 7).

Place the potatoes on a large sheet pan and add a drizzle of oil and a few pinches of salt and pepper. Toss to coat on all sides, then spread the potatoes across the sheet pan in a single layer. Roast for about 25 minutes, or until fork-tender.

To make the foraged mushrooms: Place a large skillet over medium-high heat and drizzle in the oil. Add the mushrooms in a single layer and cook for 2 minutes, undisturbed. Stir the mushrooms and cook, undisturbed, for 2 minutes more. Reduce the heat to medium and continue cooking for 4 to 6 minutes until all the liquid has evaporated and the mushrooms are brown on all sides. Season with salt and pepper to taste, then keep warm until ready to serve.

To make the salmon: Pat the salmon dry with paper towels and season generously with salt and pepper. Line a plate with paper towels.

Add enough oil to thinly coat the bottom of a large skillet and heat it over medium-high heat until the oil is shimmering. Just before adding the fish, reduce the heat to medium-low. Place two fillets in the skillet, skin-side down, and cook for 5 to 7 minutes, undisturbed, until the skin is crisp and a thermometer inserted into the thickest part of the flesh registers 120°F (49°C) for medium-rare. Gently flip the fillets and cook for about 15 seconds. Transfer to the prepared plate.

Reheat the oil, then repeat the process to cook the remaining two fillets.

To assemble, in a large bowl, toss the mushrooms and potatoes with half the dandelion pistou to evenly coat. Divide the vegetables among four plates. Garnish with pineapple weed and wild sorrel (if using), or other foraged herbs. Place each salmon fillet over the vegetables, skin-side down, and top with a few spoonfuls of onion gastrique before serving.

Leftover pistou can be refrigerated for up to 1 week, and leftover gastrique can be refrigerated for 2 weeks for other uses.

BUFFALO SHEPHERD'S PIE

It might seem strange to find bison on the menu at Glacier Bay Lodge, especially a menu dominated by salmon, halibut, and Dungeness crab—all local specialties found in and around the tidewater glaciers and deep fjords of Glacier Bay. But if you think about it, Alaskans in the bush rely heavily on the flora and fauna (not to mention their pantry staples) to get through long, cold winters, and shepherd's pie is as cozy as sherpa slippers in front of a wood-burning fire. This rustic one-pot meal is essentially a hearty meat filling doused in gravy and topped with fluffy mashed potatoes. Shepherd's pie is to red meat what potpie is to poultry.

Which leads me to ask: Since shepherd's pie is traditionally made with lamb (hence the name), if there's no lamb, can it still be called shepherd's pie? Ironically, the savory pie served at the Fairweather Dining Room uses Wyoming-bred bison, but if you want to take this recipe fully Alaskan, you can use moose or caribou (or even bear) instead. This is my version of their buffalo shepherd's pie, spiced with my "secret ingredients" (cinnamon and nutmeg—trust me on it). The dish is plenty filling on its own, but I like to serve it with a loaf of crusty bread (plus the wine I pop open for the recipe).

GLACIER BAY
NATIONAL PARK

MAKES FIVE SERVINGS

INGREDIENTS

FOR MASHED POTATOES

2 pounds (908 g) russet potatoes, peeled and cut into 1-inch (2.5 cm) dice

1 tablespoon (15 g) kosher salt

¾ cup (180 ml) milk

⅓ cup (27 g) shredded Asiago cheese

3 tablespoons (42 g) butter, at room temperature

2 garlic cloves, crushed

1 egg yolk

FOR MEAT FILLING

1 tablespoon (15 ml) olive oil

1 pound (454 g) ground bison

1 cup (160 g) diced onion

1 cup (130 g) diced carrot

1 cup (120 g) diced celery

4 garlic cloves, minced

½ teaspoon kosher salt

2 tablespoons (15 g) all-purpose flour

¼ teaspoon ground cinnamon

¼ teaspoon ground nutmeg

1 cup (240 ml) beef broth

½ cup (120 ml) dry red wine

2 tablespoons (32 g) tomato paste

1 tablespoon (15 ml) Worcestershire sauce

1 teaspoon Italian seasoning

1¼ cups (162.5 g) frozen peas, thawed

¼ cup (25 g) grated parmesan cheese

Chopped fresh parsley for garnishing

INSTRUCTIONS

To make the mashed potatoes: Place the potatoes in a large pot. Add the salt and enough water to cover the potatoes by 1 inch (2.5 cm) and bring to a boil. Reduce the heat to a rapid simmer and cook for 12 to 15 minutes until the potatoes are tender. Drain the potatoes and return them to the pot. Add the milk, cheese, butter, and garlic and mash the potatoes until smooth and creamy. Stir in the egg yolk until well combined.

recipe continues

AT-HOME TIP

If you don't have a Dutch oven, cook the meat filling in a large skillet, then transfer to a greased baking dish and top with the mashed potatoes before baking.

To make the meat filling: Preheat the oven to 400°F (200°C or gas mark 6).

In a Dutch oven over medium–high heat, swirl in the oil, add the bison and crumble the meat using a large spoon. Cook for about 5 minutes until browned, stirring occasionally. Add the onion, carrot, celery, garlic, and salt and cook for 5 to 7 minutes, stirring occasionally, until the vegetables are tender. Sprinkle the flour, cinnamon, and nutmeg over the meat mixture and stir to combine. Add the broth, wine, tomato paste, Worcestershire sauce, and Italian seasoning and bring

to a boil, stirring to coat the mixture evenly with all the seasonings. Reduce the heat to maintain a simmer and cook for about 10 minutes until the gravy is thick. Stir in the peas.

To assemble the pie: Drop large dollops of mashed potatoes over the meat mixture and smooth them out to cover. Scatter the parmesan on top.

Bake for 25 minutes until the potatoes start to turn golden brown. Garnish with parsley before serving.

ACKNOWLEDGMENTS

This book never would have happened without my editor, Thom O'Hearn, giving me a call one day with a novel idea for my next cookbook. Thank you for your encouragement and your trust in me to turn an abstract concept into my absolute favorite project to date.

A shout-out to all the chefs, proprietors, parks, and PR teams who contributed recipes—many thanks for your willingness to share your "secrets," stories, and processes and for helping me bring this book to life. I'm so inspired by what you do, and my wish list of places to visit has grown tenfold.

Sincerest thanks to all the good people who have bought, shared, reviewed, and cooked from my books, continued to spread the word about them, and added my recipes to your family dinner rotations. It's an honor to be a part of your table.

To my parents, who instilled in me a passion for food and a zest for life that have made me who I am and gotten me where I am. Thank you for supporting my whimsies and allowing me to explore and carve my own path.

And last—but certainly not least—immeasurable gratitude and love to my rock, my right-hand, road-tripping partner, and everything that's beautiful about this book—my husband, photographer, and king of the road, Will Taylor. Your incredible talent, brilliant navigation, and epic dedication to getting the perfect shot (oftentimes before sunrise) made *The National Parks Cookbook* better than I could've imagined. I'm so glad you're my co-captain in this crazy, awesome journey.

ABOUT THE AUTHOR

Linda Ly grew up in a family that lived for good food and great road trips, which inspired her lifelong love of cooking and traveling—a love that has influenced her writing on her award-winning blog, *Garden Betty*, and several farm-to-table and outdoor cookbooks, including *The No-Waste Vegetable Cookbook*, *The Backyard Fire Cookbook*, and bestseller *The New Camp Cookbook*.

As of 2022, Linda has visited more than two dozen national parks—along with many national monuments, seashores, parkways, and other National Park System units—but a far-flung dream is to drive up the Alaska Highway and visit all eight of Alaska's national parks.

Linda lives on a sunny homestead in Bend, Oregon, where she's getting a food forest off (or should we say, *in*) the ground with her husband, Will, and their daughters Gemma and Ember. The family is always on the hunt for their next adventure as they go Onewheeling, snowboarding, surfskating, mountain biking, hiking, paddling, and exploring the country in their twenty-four-foot (7.3 m) Minnie Winnie named Wanda (as in "wanda lust").

Read more at www.gardenbetty.com.

ABOUT THE PHOTOGRAPHER

From an early age, Will Taylor was captivated by photography and took pictures with anything he could get his hands on, from disposable cameras to his parents' vintage Rolleiflex. But it was the ten years spent "living the life" in Lake Tahoe, California, and being surrounded by spectacular scenery every day that ignited his passion for storytelling and motivated him to make a career out of photography.

For the past thirty years, Will's assignments in landscapes, lifestyle, fashion, and food have taken him around the world and have appeared in dozens of publications, including his wife Linda's cookbooks.

After the birth of his first daughter, he and Linda left the urban sprawl of Southern California for rural life in Central Oregon. They spend as much time as possible outside, playing in the Cascades and showing their two little girls the joys of chasing sunsets off the beaten path.

CONTRIBUTORS AND FEATURED NATIONAL PARKS

CONTRIBUTORS

CAMP DENALI (DENALI NATIONAL PARK)
www.campdenali.com

CHULITNA LODGE (LAKE CLARK NATIONAL PARK)
www.chulitnalodge.com

GLACIER PARK LODGE (GLACIER NATIONAL PARK)
www.glacierparkcollection.com/lodging/
glacier-park-lodge

KALALOCH LODGE (OLYMPIC NATIONAL PARK)
www.thekalalochlodge.com

KENAI FJORDS WILDERNESS LODGE (KENAI FJORDS NATIONAL PARK)
www.kenaifjordswildernesslodge.com

MAMMOTH HOT SPRINGS HOTEL (YELLOWSTONE NATIONAL PARK)
www.yellowstonenationalparklodges.
com/dining

MCCARTHY LODGE (WRANGELL-ST. ELIAS NATIONAL PARK)
www.mccarthylodge.com

OLD FAITHFUL SNOW LODGE (YELLOWSTONE NATIONAL PARK)
www.yellowstonenationalparklodges.
com/dining

PARADISE INN (MT. RAINIER NATIONAL PARK)
www.mtrainierguestservices.com/
paradiseinndining

REDOUBT MOUNTAIN LODGE (LAKE CLARK NATIONAL PARK)
www.redoubtlodge.com

ROOSEVELT LODGE (YELLOWSTONE NATIONAL PARK)
www.yellowstonenationalparklodges.
com/dining

SILVER SALMON CREEK LODGE (LAKE CLARK NATIONAL PARK)
www.silversalmoncreek.com

FEATURED NATIONAL PARKS

ACADIA NATIONAL PARK
www.nps.gov/acad

BADLANDS NATIONAL PARK
www.nps.gov/badl

BISCAYNE NATIONAL PARK
www.nps.gov/bisc

BRYCE CANYON NATIONAL PARK
www.nps.gov/brca

CAPITOL REEF NATIONAL PARK
www.nps.gov/care

CARLSBAD CAVERNS NATIONAL PARK
www.nps.gov/cave

CONGAREE NATIONAL PARK
www.nps.gov/cong

CRATER LAKE NATIONAL PARK
www.nps.gov/crla

CUYAHOGA VALLEY NATIONAL PARK
www.nps.gov/cuva

DEATH VALLEY NATIONAL PARK
www.nps.gov/deva

DENALI NATIONAL PARK
www.nps.gov/dena

GLACIER BAY NATIONAL PARK
www.nps.gov/glba

SKYLAND (SHENANDOAH NATIONAL PARK)
www.goshenandoah.com/lodging/skyland

THE AHWAHNEE (YOSEMITE NATIONAL PARK)
www.travelyosemite.com/lodging/
the-ahwahnee

THE INN AT BRANDYWINE FALLS (CUYAHOGA VALLEY NATIONAL PARK)
www.innatbrandywinefalls.com

WUKSACHI LODGE (SEQUOIA NATIONAL PARK)
www.visitsequoia.com/lodging/
wuksachi-lodge

GLACIER NATIONAL PARK
www.nps.gov/glac

GRAND CANYON NATIONAL PARK
www.nps.gov/grca

GRAND TETON NATIONAL PARK
www.nps.gov/grte

**GREAT SMOKY MOUNTAINS
NATIONAL PARK**
www.nps.gov/grsm

INDIANA DUNES NATIONAL PARK
www.nps.gov/indu

ISLE ROYALE NATIONAL PARK
www.nps.gov/isro

JOSHUA TREE NATIONAL PARK
www.nps.gov/jotr

KENAI FJORDS NATIONAL PARK
www.nps.gov/kefj

LAKE CLARK NATIONAL PARK
www.nps.gov/lacl

MAMMOTH CAVE NATIONAL PARK
www.nps.gov/maca

MESA VERDE NATIONAL PARK
www.nps.gov/meve

MT. RAINIER NATIONAL PARK
www.nps.gov/mora

NEW RIVER GORGE NATIONAL PARK
www.nps.gov/neri

OLYMPIC NATIONAL PARK
www.nps.gov/olym

ROCKY MOUNTAIN NATIONAL PARK
www.nps.gov/romo

SAGUARO NATIONAL PARK
www.nps.gov/sagu

SEQUOIA NATIONAL PARK
www.nps.gov/seki

SHENANDOAH NATIONAL PARK
www.nps.gov/shen

VIRGIN ISLANDS NATIONAL PARK
www.nps.gov/viis

VOYAGEURS NATIONAL PARK
www.nps.gov/voya

WRANGELL-ST. ELIAS NATIONAL PARK
www.nps.gov/wrst

YELLOWSTONE NATIONAL PARK
www.nps.gov/yell

YOSEMITE NATIONAL PARK
www.nps.gov/yose

ZION NATIONAL PARK
www.nps.gov/zion

INDEX